A MOST DANGEROUS
JOURNEY

A MOST DANGEROUS
JOURNEY

THE LIFE OF AN AFRICAN ELEPHANT

ROGER A. CARAS

WITH PHOTOGRAPHS
BY THE AUTHOR

DIAL BOOKS · NEW YORK

Published by Dial Books
A Division of Penguin Books USA Inc.
375 Hudson Street
New York, New York 10014

Copyright © 1995 by Roger A. Caras
All rights reserved
Designed by Julie Rauer
Printed in the U.S.A.
First Edition
1 3 5 7 9 10 8 6 4 2

Library of Congress Cataloging in Publication Data
Caras, Roger A.
A most dangerous journey: the life of an African elephant/
by Roger A. Caras / with photographs by the author—1st ed.
p. cm.
ISBN 0-8037-1880-2
1. African elephant—Juvenile literature. [1. African elephant.
2. Elephants. 3. Endangered species.] I. Title.
QL737.P98C35 1995 599.4'1—dc20 95-2548 CIP AC

Frontispiece: A full-grown African elephant may be thirteen feet tall at the shoulder and weigh up to six and a half tons. **p. 192** A herd of wildebeests, also called white-bearded gnus, grazes on a plain. **p. 193** The eland, standing, is the largest antelope in the world. Nearby, lying down, is a young Thomson's gazelle, one of the smallest antelopes. **p. 194** A giraffe eats leaves from the higher branches. **p. 195** A waterbuck has long, curved horns.
p. 196 A lioness and her cub rest on a rock.

THE AFRICAN ELEPHANT

ORDER:

Proboscidea

FAMILY:

ELEPHANTIDAE

GENUS:

Loxodonta

SPECIES:

L. africana (Ndovu)—bush or large-eared elephant
L. cyclotis—forest or round-eared elephant
L. pumilio—pgymy elephant

Note: The existence of the pygmy elephant as a separate
species is not widely and certainly not generally accepted.
Whether all African elephants, in fact, belong in the single
umbrella species Loxodonta africana is open
to a great deal of argument.

This book is for Seymour Reiknecht, Esq.
and he knows why.
And for Amanda Blake.

AUTHOR'S NOTE

Fifty years ago it was estimated that there were perhaps four or five million elephants in Africa. Today, they number only in the thousands, and that soon will not be enough to ensure their survival.

The elephant is disappearing for several reasons. There is that fatal disease that nearly all elephants get. It is called ivory and it is getting far too close to being one hundred percent fatal. We are in need of an ethic that says *Thou shalt not misuse living creatures*. Until we have it and it is as ingrained as is our ethical rejection of cannibalism, slavery, and human sacrifice, we shall see animals abused, misused, and they will vanish.

The other critical factor is that elephants are terrible neighbors if you happen to be in agriculture. They are difficult, demanding animals that evolved very specifically to survive over huge areas with enormous amounts of food and water. The governments of Africa must decide whether tourism is important enough to them to create the infrastructure to support an elephant population, and whether an environmental ethic can be established. Whatever decision is made, the existence of this most magnificent species will depend upon it.

CONTENTS

ACKNOWLEDGMENTS

A book is not born in a typewriter or a word processor. It is part of the fabric of its author's life. Whatever, whoever contributes to that fabric is a part of the book that results.

My life has been an exotic one in many ways. I have made twenty-five trips to Africa, many journeys to Asia, the Arctic, Antarctic, the Amazon, gone to Europe endlessly, and have taken trips time and again to the Galápagos Islands. Every journey in Africa has been shared by Jill, my wife of thirty-nine years. Pamela and Clay, our daughter and son, each accompanied us eight times and we looked at elephants together. Looking at elephants as they are in the wild is a kind of Caras family "thing." How many elephants have there been? I lost count years ago. But collectively, in Kenya, Tanzania, Zimbabwe, and South Africa, thousands, a good many thousands. And that does not count the herds observed again and again in Sri Lanka, née Ceylon. But those were of a different species. Ndovu is an African elephant.

Acknowledged, then, with love, Jill, Pamela, Clay, and our friends the elephants. It has been an unbeatable combination.

To many friends here and in Africa, living for the most part, but some, I regret, now dead, thank you for sharing Africa and Ndovu with me. The late, beloved Amanda Blake comes to mind first and perhaps foremost. Her profound love of the great beasts, shared with us year after year as we journeyed together in Africa, brought them into ever sharper focus.

To everyone who has written about the elephant, to the photographers and artists who have captured majestic images of this greatest of all land animals, thank you. I have studied your work and know much of it well. From Guy Coheleach to Cynthia Moss, there have been people who have captured both the detail and the essence of the elephant in ways distinctly their own, ways suited to their special skills. Their insights have been invaluable, in fact, indispensable.

There are many angles from which a writer must approach his elephant, many ways he must come to know him. Our knowledge of anything so vast and wonderful is a combination of the many ways we gain our impressions. Each matters, for each links with all of the others. And each is hereby acknowledged. Ndovu is the sum of all those linked impressions and all of the individual elephants that can come in one writer's lifetime.   R A C

1

THE BIRTH
OF NDOVU

The cow had been uneasy all that day and much of the night before. She was uncomfortable and apparently anxious and she stayed apart from the rest of the herd. That was unusual, because she was naturally one of the most  social animals. Like all elephants she needed the scent, the sound, and especially the touch of her own kind to feel secure. Touch was so important that no member of the herd ever missed an opportunity to rub against another, caress, or just reach out with their trunk and make even the briefest of contacts. Her eyesight was only fair, but she was reassured by the sight of her herd mates too. She always traveled in the company of other cows, their calves, and half-grown young. Their familiar smells and their audible stomach rumblings completed her sense of well-being. That was basic. Everything flowed from that.

Near dusk the cow became increasingly restless and began moving toward a cut in the hills where the shadows had begun to form. It was almost as dark as it would get among the trees. Not until dawn would the first rays of the newly risen sun begin another light show over the Mara Masai. For now, a blanket of stars would provide pinpoints of light. It is like this near the equator in Africa.

The cow had mated with a huge bull over twenty-one months earlier and the time to give birth had finally come. The cow did not move away from the herd by herself. Her daughter, born eight years ago, two of her sisters, and an old aunt followed at a discreet distance. There had been no signal between them. They each had been watching the pregnant cow for days and she had been giving quiet cues that her time was near. The closeness in which elephants live appears to give them insights into each other that defy our understanding. That insight was sharpened by their concern, which was part of the herd and of each animal in it. And now another elephant was about to enter the world and the guardians would stand watch.

As they approached the small valley the cow had chosen, one of her sisters explored a slight breeze with her trunk and caught the unmistakable odor of cat urine. The movement of air had been so soft, so slight, it barely moved the grass but it reeked of ammonia. The alerted cow shrilled a warning sound and began moving in the direction from which the scent had come. Lions were near and would have to be killed or driven off. They would never be tolerated anywhere in the vicinity of the cow when she was about to give birth.

The other cows began moving in circles, their ears spread wide to make themselves appear even more intimidating than they were and to listen for any small sound. They grumbled and shrilled to each other, shattering the dusk with noise. However, the blast from the sister who had first caught their scent had been enough to warn the lions. Three young males had been asleep near the opening to the valley between the hills. They were sleeping off an orgy of feeding on a zebra they had killed just before dawn that same morning. They had spent most of the day gorging on rich red muscle meat, the hide, the vegetable content of the zebra's gut, and especially their prey's organs. When the warning blast came from the cow who detected their presence, they had stumbled over each other in their efforts to get away. Before the cows began systematically beating the bush, moving in widening circles, exploring every odor on the wind, the cats were almost a mile away and still moving fast. There was no dignity in their retreat, just a good sense of survival.

A newborn elephant calf is at its most vulnerable stage. But few get taken as prey because they are so closely guarded by their mothers and the other members of the herd. The larger cats, leopard and especially lion, and other major predators, like hyenas and hunting dogs, are never tolerated in the area of young elephants, especially the newborn. All predators heed the elephant's size, its intelligence, and its cooperative social structure. In Africa the elephant, not the lion, is king.

The cow moved onto a flat area near a small pond. There were signs of previous elephant activity everywhere. Trees were down as if struck by a tornado, and those that still stood were debarked and dead. Most of the grass had been pulled up in clumps and the soft-textured reeds at the edge of the pond lay flattened along the paths made by huge bodies pushing toward the water. It was an area of intense use because it was secluded and there was water and perpetually renewing vegetation. It was a good place to live, a fine place to be born.

A single cobra, almost five and a half feet long, was exposed in an open area of dust as the elephants approached. Although they moved quietly, he felt the vibrations of their great weight, and vanished into a half-dead bush. Less than a minute later he emerged on the far side and slid twenty feet more to a termite hill and disappeared into one of its red earth funnels. In seconds he was moving down through silent passageways, as hard as cement, that led to a labyrinth of chambers and connecting galleys forty feet underground. It was a secret world unknown even to the elephants who were now overhead. The cobra and the elephants would not confront each other if either could avoid it.

Black-faced vervet monkeys in the trees chittered and chattered to one another on the arrival of the elephants and took to the higher branches. They ran along them, reaching out to one another, pushing, mock fighting, slipping, falling, catching onto lower branches, then climbing higher again. The elephants ignored them and would heed them only if they issued anxious warning sounds that could mean predators were in the area. But for the most part the elephants depended on their own hearing and keen sense of smell to keep the place where the new calf would be born safe from intruders.

4

In a matter of minutes after the small herd of elephants arrived, every monkey in the vicinity was asleep. No monkey on the African continent outlasts the sun. None are active at night unless a python or leopard attacks the band sleeping in the trees. Then they fuss for only a few minutes, and sleep again.

From a termite nest not more than fifty feet from the one into which the retreating cobra had vanished, pygmy mongooses began to appear. Within three minutes, twelve of the excited little hunters emerged and began looking around for anything small enough for them to eat. They fairly trembled with energy, ready to fight and kill. They rattled the dry leaves and disturbed weed clumps near where the cow elephant stood, but she heard their sounds and knew that these mites of energy could not harm her calf.

In Africa more than the sun sets. Diurnal animals, those that are active during the day, like the vervet monkeys, sleep at night while the nocturnal animals such as bush babies appear to take their place. At dawn and dusk, the merging of night and day, an overlapping group of animals, the crepuscular or twilight species, inherits the world. The cats, although they hunt anytime they are hungry, are most active in these cooler hours as are hyenas, many snakes, and the smaller cats, and the pygmy mongoose's larger kin, the civets and genets. The sounds change at these times too. Dawn and dusk in Africa sound like different worlds, for indeed that is what they are.

The cow slipped through the papyrus and other waterside plants when the evening sounds were at their peak. It was as if a large orchestra were tuning up, but the sounds offered no threat to the cow.

She stood in the water up to her belly, swayed a little, moaned, squirted water into her throat with her trunk, and then came back up onto dry land. Pulling a few leaves off a tree, she munched on them, and seemed to shiver. She poked at the dry sand with one huge front foot, then the other. She turned around several times in place, flapped her ears, then appeared to brace herself. She spread her hind legs slightly and leaned forward. She moaned, and her alert attendants responded with soft answers as they circled her, but not too closely. They were almost as restless as the cow herself had been when she left the herd. Now, in fact, she was calmer than they were. The first birth, for there were to be twins, took just over thirty minutes. A female calf fell to the earth behind her mother, who was still standing. The calf was dying. She landed headfirst and then fell sideways. She would breathe only a few times, then expire. The umbilical cord came apart and the cow gently nudged the dead calf with her foot to free it of the placenta that still partially shrouded her. There was no response, and after waiting patiently the cow poked the calf lightly with a tusk, tried to pry her free of the ground. When there was still no effort on the calf's part to move or rise, her mother tried with her trunk. Then the cow appeared to understand, in the way that elephants do, and her attendants did as well.

But now another baby was about to be born. The cow again felt stirrings deep inside of her, far stronger than a natural settling down after the birth of the dead calf. The birth process was starting up again.

The second calf, a bull, was born forty-five minutes after his sister and weighed 234 pounds. He too landed headfirst, jerking apart the umbilical cord.

This calf was active and strong. While the cow scraped away the placenta, the little bull-calf's legs were working, awkwardly paddling against the unfamiliar air. Within minutes of being born, *Ndovu* (the Masai name for elephant) was struggling to lift his head off the ground. The cow worked the two placentas into the dust and used her feet to shove sand and vegetation over them.

In just a little over an hour Ndovu stood. He was wobbly, had poor balance, and had almost no control over his trunk. What he would eventually use like a surgical instrument, despite its size and ponderous shape, now wagged like a huge, misplaced, and altogether useless finger. His ears were plastered flat against his neck, and his body was covered with dark hairs that would fall away in the weeks ahead.

Well before the first hint of the sun splashed to the east across the cloudless sky, Ndovu nursed. He thrust up against one of his mother's two breasts between her front legs. His trunk flopped sideways, out of the way, and Ndovu pulled greedily and with great vigor. He would live, and he would eventually grow to massive proportions.

Because she had never bonded with the first calf, the cow paid little attention to her. Twice during the night she wandered over to examine the body briefly. Then she became totally involved with Ndovu, as she now would be for years. The bonding between them was quick in coming. She stood with her back to the dead

An infant calf stays close to his mother, who will protect him from danger until he is able to protect himself. ❖

A three-month-old calf nuzzles a half-grown elephant while two cows watch over them. ❖

calf while Ndovu fed. It was then that the cow's older daughter quietly shoved the body of the first calf away into the brush and pulled branches down over her, keening softly as she did so. Ndovu, the survivor, tugged and nursed, demanding to be fed and nurtured.

2

THE PLAYTHING

By the time Ndovu had lived through his first dawn, he was about to become a member of the herd. A distinctly elephant ritual, this was essential for his survival.

After he had successfully nursed for the first time, each of the four  attending cows, his half sister, his two aunts, and his great- aunt, came to him one at a time. His mother watched while each cow ran her trunk over Ndovu. There was no part of him that they did not caress and smell. He was joined to each of them during those moments, and through them to their herd. It was all done in under an hour. From then on he could run to any of them if his mother was not immediately at hand, and find protection. He was now linked to them in a way that has its parallels in other species, but is never quite the same. Lions are social, but males are likely to be cannibals and eat their own cubs when other food is in short supply. Gorillas, chimpanzees, and human beings are social, but not as reliable around all the young in their social unit as elephants are. Elephants do not hurt their own young. In that way they are different from many of the higher mammals.

Later that first day the cow's two sisters left, going back to the herd gathered near a river two miles from the place where Ndovu was born. Within minutes the other animals in the herd knew what had happened. The smell of a newborn bull calf was on the returning cows.

Back near the pond the cow stood patiently while Ndovu hid beneath her belly. He nursed frequently, and although it was not yet apparent, he had started to grow. Perhaps, more accurately, he continued to grow as he had inside his mother. Periodically he lay on his side and slept in his mother's shadow while her daughter and aunt munched on leaves from the nearby trees. An elephant's digestive system is very inefficient. No more than fifty percent of the food taken in is used. The rest passes through undigested. It was necessary, then, for each of the cows, including Ndovu's mother, to eat between three and four hundred pounds of vegetation every twenty-four hours in order to maintain a good condition. That involved virtually constant eating, which is something all elephants do. Each of the guardians made three trips down to the pond, waded in, and drank about sixty gallons of water in that one day. That too was normal consumption. An elephant is a very demanding tenant on the land.

The cow moved down to the edge of the reeds with her infant at her side and left him there while she moved into the pond to drink. Her two attendants were never more than a few feet away, and when her aunt blasted a warning, the new mother came out of the water in a matter of seconds. About a thousand yards away a leopard was moving through the bush, and a strong gust of wind brought news of him to the pond. Instantly all three cows were on full alert, facing the direction from which the wind had come. Their trunks were outstretched, anxiously testing, tasting for more news. But the leopard had other matters to attend to. She was a transient and wouldn't risk an encounter with the elephants. In any event, there is nothing to be gained in a confrontation between a leopard and three cow elephants. Some of the most important lessons a wild animal must learn is which animals to avoid and which may be challenged. The elephant alone may challenge all.

But the leopard was soon gone and the elephants stood down. There was no danger, and within the hour the cow left her calf under the gaze of others and returned to the pond to drink. She ate too, and came back to her calf who was anxious to nurse again.

About midafternoon on the calf's first day the cobra who had been in the clearing when the mother and guardians first arrived emerged from the termite mound and began moving away from the elephants toward another marshy area where he was likely to find prey in the form of a rabbit or a hare. From the moment his head first appeared in the mouth of the chimney, he had not quite five minutes left to live. On a low branch of a tree eighty feet away, a strange bird stood watching on stiltlike legs. She was a secretary bird, an aberrant eagle with a family, *Sagittariidae*, all to herself. Cobras were her normal fare, all snakes and lizards in fact were, and her eyesight was extremely sharp. She saw the snake and watched him start away, then she dropped off the branch and took flight. Silently she glided over toward the snake, who somehow detected the threat. He whirled and reared, spreading the ribs behind his head, creating the characteristic hood for which cobras are known. The hood is meant to intimidate, but the secretary bird was not impressed. She intended to kill the cobra, despite his size and his formidable supply of venom, and deliver him to her nest for her chicks to eat. She stalked toward the snake and he struck out, trying to bury his fangs in the bird's slender legs. She danced, spread her wings, rose, landed even nearer than before, and stomped the snake with a powerful taloned foot, injuring him badly. Again the snake struck, was stomped again, writhed, but was unable to counter the assault. In minutes the snake was dead, although nerve reflexes kept him twitching as though he were alive. The secretary bird bit him behind the neck, severing his backbone. She grabbed him midbody with her beak and beat away on a running takeoff, the snake dangling from her beak. Within minutes her young were feeding.

Nearby Ndovu, unconcerned, nursed yet again. Almost every minute of his life, as a member of the African wildlife community, would be filled with dramas like the brief battle between the cobra and the secretary bird. Ndovu would pay little attention to most of it because his eyes made him a poor spectator. He would register best what he could smell and hear. Elephants pay very close attention to one another, but relatively little to other animals except to the larger predators that might be dangerous to their young. They are peaceful and generally tolerant of other animals. When there is a newborn calf, however, they are tense and alert and can be unforgiving.

There was a second snake nearby, intent on finding his meal. A magnificent rock python just over twenty-three feet long, he waited for a gazelle or antelope to pass beneath his perch on a branch of a yellow fever tree. He would drop on his unsuspecting prey, bear it to earth with his tremendous weight of close to three hundred pounds, and then envelop it in his coils. He would suffocate the animal, then swallow it headfirst. His skin glistened in the bars of light that came through the trees and caught him as he lay upon the branch. The front five feet of his body dangled down like an inverted periscope, and he scanned the bush for promising movement.

He sensed and then saw the elephant, but he was too slow in reacting. The cow's trunk caught him just behind the head and with a ferocious heave he was ripped away from his perch. His entire length snapped through the air like a whip and he was smashed against the trunk of the tree in which he had been waiting. The cow started away, but then turned back and drove her tusks, one then the other then both, into the snake's body. So often dreaded by man, snakes are fragile creatures whose bones are easily broken and that are frequently beset by fatal infections from even the slightest wound. The giant snake would not have bothered Ndovu, but in their hypercautious way, the cows were intolerant of anything that came near them. Twice they drove away small bands of impala—graceful, inoffensive vegetarians that could pose no possible threat to them.

And so Ndovu passed his first full day and faced his second night. The next time the sun moved, like a curtain of fire across the surface of the pond, the three cows and the calf would be gone, moving back toward the herd. Only part of what an elephant must do to survive and reproduce is inherited behavior. Like all of the highly intelligent species in the wildlife world, there was much that Ndovu had to learn, and his herd was his schoolroom, a learning center with more teachers than pupils.

The herd watched as the cow and her calf and her two remaining attendants came out from behind the curtain of trees and began moving into their unit. More accurately, the herd members smelled them, then heard them; the cow was rumbling a low moaning sound as she moved forward. Then, at almost the last minute, they saw the returnees and the newcomer. There was intense interest and the scattered animals began moving as the cow and her calf stood waiting.

The herd soon started north to a river they knew was there, and one by one its members got near enough to the calf to examine him with their trunks. The baby was thus registered and the herd was his family forever.

One young bull in the herd had reached nine years and was beginning to be a problem. He had engaged each of the other young males in shoving contests, forehead to forehead, twining trunks with each and pulling. The young bulls had short, stubby tusks and had thrust at one another, inflicting some pain but never really fighting seriously.

Soon after a new calf is born, the other members of the herd smell and touch him, forming a strong, protective bond. ❖

There were days when the contests became tiresome, and the older cows were getting cross. At times the youngsters were sent away when an old cow threatened them. However cocky the young males were with each other, they knew that the mature cows could be dangerous, especially when calves were around.

As the herd moved toward the north, the biggest of the young bulls challenged another young male about his own age. They locked trunks and began moving their forequarters from side to side, clashing their small tusks, shoving each other, butting each other in play that had a higher purpose as well. At one point the alpha, or dominant, male caught his opponent off guard and hit him in his side in a heavy, thumping impact. The young male stumbled away and crashed into Ndovu's mother, sending the little calf squealing to a position of safety under her belly. In a moment or two he was nursing.

However, the other cows in the herd closed in on the two delinquents in a way that left no doubt as to what was going to happen. The young bulls had crossed a forbidden line, they were a danger to the very young and they had to go. They backed away, then turned and walked off without argument. They were now banished outcasts and would have to find a solitary bull and become his *askaris*, or guards. Or else they would live alone. Six of the cows followed them for almost a mile and then went back to the herd.

❖ ❖ ❖

Ndovu's third night was about to begin. In single file, except when a cow had young, the herd of twenty-three elephants moved toward the setting sun, creating around each animal a halo of many colors. From behind stacks of puffed white clouds, fingers of color—lavender and green, gold, silver, and brilliant pink—shot across the sky like arrows pointing east to where the next day would begin after a star-spangled black night had come and gone. It was an equatorial sunset, among the most magnificent in the world, filtered through shades of color that otherwise surely do not exist. Marabou storks and vultures had come to rest on the tops of the umbrella-shaped trees of the savannah. Millions of smaller birds had already found night roosts and hunkered down against a drop in temperature that was certain to come. In the wooded places the vervet monkeys and olive baboons had settled in for the night and the eagle-owls were stirring, preparing for their evening hunt.

In a burrow near the line of the elephants' march, two spotted hyena cubs were born. Their mother had been carrying them for one hundred and twenty days. Very shortly after emerging into the world, they nursed. Both would live. A leopard-sized cheetah worried about her three cubs as the hyena troop emerged—sixteen adults and seven partially grown cubs—and cackled into night. When the sun rose, the cheetah would have one cub left of her three. She would move him away from this high-risk area and would live to see him grow to adulthood. When the hyenas roamed the night and made their threatening sounds, most animals in the area had reason to fear. Hyenas have enormously powerful jaws and more often than not kill their own prey. In fact, lions often scavenge what hyenas leave, and fear them as they do few other animals. When a lion grows old, the hyenas watch. When a lion is injured or feeble, the

A spotted hyena hunts other animals for food, but is usually no threat to an elephant. ❖

hyenas close in. These particular hyenas, however, would not concern Ndovu, unless he happened to be caught alone in the early days of his life, and that was not likely to happen.

The sun was down. The night sounds had started. The grass bent over as a cool breeze moved across the savannah. Ndovu moved a little closer to his mother and she stopped. The other cows stopped too, and pulled out clumps of grass to feed on. Ndovu leaned against his mother's leg and slipped down until he was on his side. He would sleep as his mother stood towering over him. Her herd mates would allow for Ndovu's needs in these early days of life. They would listen for intrusion or threat. Ndovu's sleep was without fear. His herd saw to that.

3

FIRST LESSONS

The open savannah, or grassland, where the herd spent the night was peaceful for the elephants, for a lone rhinoceros bull grazing a mile to the south, and for a herd of cape buffalo two miles to the west. For the other animals these were  anxious hours.

That night a three-thousand-pound giraffe was killed by six lions who banded together and attacked it. Not far away an elderly lion, whose jaw had been shattered by the kick of a zebra stallion he had been hunting, had himself been killed by hyenas.

But death is matched by new life. Seven lion cubs were born to two prides within a few miles of where the old male had died. Sunrise found two giraffe cows even closer to the elephant herd, working the placenta away from their newborn calves. Thousands of birds' eggs would hatch that day, and in-

A lioness rests on a high rock where she can observe other animals (possible prey) below her. ❖

sects and their kin would appear by uncountable millions.

Overhead, three thousand European white storks, coming from their range in northern Europe that stretched east to Siberia, headed for a grassy area not far in front of the elephants. Having survived their migration, they would live for another summer south of the equator while their northern nesting range lay under blankets of snow. Relatively few cranes had been lost along the way. A few had been shot by sportsmen, supposedly warming up for a waterfowl hunt.

Elephants don't generally school their young except in how to act toward other members of the herd, but they do teach by example. Within a few days of his birth Ndovu would begin watching, listening to, and smelling the older animals. He would learn to react as they reacted. What upset them, what attracted them, what made them curious would affect him in the same ways as he grew. When he became an adult, he would be like them in almost every way. His few individual characteristics would involve his level of aggression, and therefore his dominance and intelligence. Few signs of either aggressiveness or intelligence were apparent in these first days, but both traits would develop as Ndovu grew.

A few days after the herd began to move, a grass fire triggered by lightning flared up. The fire was behind the herd and moving toward it. In minutes the elephants caught the scent from the erratic breezes that meandered and gusted over the grassy knolls and slopes. The herd hurried onward. Elephants cannot run, nor can they jump. They have one gait, walking, either fast or slow. When trouble threatens they can walk thirty-five miles an hour, and that was the pace they struck at the first suggestion of smoke. They held it for a few minutes, but Ndovu quickly tired and his mother slowed down for him. The others in the herd followed suit. They came to a dry riverbed that would form a satisfactory firebreak unless a huge wind blew up and carried the fire explosively across into the brush on the far side.

Forever after that time Ndovu, who had never seen any flame, would dread its smell, because his mother and his herd had made the dreading sounds in their throats and had fled when its smell had appeared on the wind. No member of Ndovu's herd had ever seen a fire, but each one had learned from the elders that it was something to be feared, and now they had taught that to Ndovu too.

The pond near the clearing where Ndovu had been born was rapidly disappearing. The two springs that fed it had been drying up even while Ndovu and his mother were still there. Within days the only animals that could use it would be butterflies, hundreds of pale yellow and white butterflies, that would perch on little ridges in the mud beside the last of the puddles and make it seem as if the ground itself were aflutter.

The area was stricken with drought and would get worse before it got better. For elephants, whose daily water demands are great—fifty to sixty gallons per adult animal—drought is a time when the older and younger animals frequently die. All elephants suffer when there is a lack of water. Water quenches their prodigious thirst and helps them keep their body temperature stable at between ninety-six and ninety-nine degrees Fahrenheit. Water provides mud that protects elephants against biting insects and external parasites, and it supports the vegetation they need in enormous quantities. A river is a playground; a lake, a gymnasium; a marsh, a place of good feelings. An adult elephant casts off four and a half pounds of urine a day, including five and a half ounces of sodium chloride. This is necessary to maintain its healthy body chemistry, and water is needed for the task.

When ponds and rivers dry up, waterside vegetation, with its soft and pulpy stems and leaves, dies back too. This is fatal for the oldest animals. Elephants grow seven sets of teeth during their lives, and the durability of the last set defines the individual elephant's life span, which is normally fifty to seventy years. When those last teeth are worn down, largely by the hard and gritty sand that comes up with the roots of every clump of grass harvested, the elephant can no longer process food. It then becomes weak and dies. The older animals instinctively stay near water, where the pulpy plants are less demanding on their teeth. When soft food cannot be found, hundreds of pounds of it for each elephant every day, the older animals inevitably will soon die. Ndovu was aware of the anxiety of the herd. There was a sense of unrest, and the herd moved along as quickly as the young and the old could manage. A few did break away and hurry on ahead.

On the fourth night of the march away from drought, Ndovu slept under his mother's hulking form; she would stand all night to guard her infant son. Other elephants joined the herd, not as herd members but as fellow travelers seeking water. One hundred more would follow in the days ahead. The herds would keep their own members for the most part, although a few liaisons would occur. When the animals finally reached the flowing river, they would have more or less the same relationships they had had when they started out.

Ndovu's mother did not know the strange elephants, and she was more alert than ever and kept her baby close to her. If he strayed, she grumbled ominously and hooked him back to her side with her muscular trunk. On several occasions she butted other adults who were too close, using her forehead, her tusks, and her hips to maintain the space. Since Ndovu was a very new elephant, the newcomers were attracted to him. He was examined over and over again, touched, smelled, caressed. His mother tolerated mature cows, but bulls were generally warned away, especially the younger bulls who could be rough and insensitive.

One morning a very large bull came close to Ndovu and his mother, and stood watching them. He watched for ten minutes and then moved away.

The moving herds split apart in parallel streams, then came together again as the rough ground dictated. Individuals often went off with the wrong group, but they would rejoin their own herds when they reached the river.

Ndovu was nursing, as he would continue to do for the next two years. His mother's milk, tasting very much like coconut milk, was eighty-two percent water, and the baby elephant received all the moisture he needed in his food. He continued to grow and develop despite the drought. Just as his mother used her body to shield him from the sun, she protected him too from the lack of food and water around them. As long as she survived, he would survive; and she was a young, healthy, robust cow who, although she was losing weight daily, would live to lead Ndovu to the river.

The sun burned down harshly. The dust kicked up by the thousands of shuffling animals all seeking water glowed in the heat of 103 degrees Fahrenheit. The air formed swirling dust devils that careened and bobbed like miniature tornadoes.

Now the animals could smell the water. It was only sixty miles away. The first large watercourse they came to had dried up. The elephants looked for pools, but there were none on the surface. Marabou storks pecked relentlessly at the corpses of crocodiles, the last animals to die as the water evaporated. Ndovu's mother moved back and forth across the deepest dry channel where the river had run until recently. She raised the dust with great blasts from her trunk and inhaled dust and scent until she had the information she needed. There was still water below, and she began working the dust and then the soil with one front foot and then the other.

Other elephants were doing the same thing all along the deepest cuts in the riverbed. Soon the holes were two or three feet deep, and water, held underground where the sun could not reach it, began trickling in. Ndovu's mother drank, and the other elephants who had chosen their spots well drank too. Water seeped slowly into the small holes, but it did continue to come. Soon other animals, unable to dig for themselves, could smell the water and began edging in. The elephants who had not had all the water they needed drove the intruders away. Some backed off and let the other animals suck at the mud and wait for more water to trickle in.

A few elephants had actually tapped directly into an underground stream, and their holes quickly filled and overflowed onto the ground. At these spots the hoofed animals pushed in from all sides. The elephants kept at the holes for as long as they cared to, but let the overflow go to whichever animals could claim it. And then the journey began again. The water below the surface of the dry riverbed began giving out before many hours had passed.

Sixty miles away a true river ran, and wildlife flowed to its banks from hundreds of miles around. Lions crouched down and sipped cool water next to zebras, enemies forgetting to be enemies in their common need. The elephants came closer.

Beneath the surface of the water, huge forms slipped toward the banks again and again. Crocodiles, some nearly sixteen feet long, glided through the clouded currents, watching for any trace of a land animal with any part of its body in the water. They watched too for shadows that revealed animals hovering just over the water's surface. The crocodilians, whose ancestors preceded the dinosaurs, are masters of ambush. With a powerful thrust of their tails the giants launched upward and clamped their jaws on any animal within reach. A zebra leg, the face of a wildebeest, the body of an impala. As soon as they took hold, the monsters slipped back underwater with their struggling prey.

Underwater was a scene of carnage as the crocodiles, weighing a thousand pounds or more, lunged and gulped. On the banks of the river, animals at the water's edge were pushed in by others pressing from behind. Once in the water an antelope or gazelle was lucky to

When water is scarce, zebras will gather at mud holes and rivers even though lions and other enemies may also be there. ❖

get away intact. Mostly they were grabbed and eaten by the crocodiles. A twenty-foot python—perhaps excited by the crush of life so close by—hung from a branch low over the water, and a crocodile lunged upward and grasped him two feet behind his head. The python and the branch he had been hanging from crashed down into the river, dragged by the weight of the subaquatic hunter. The snake immediately began coiling around his attacker and he was freed. He pulled back and started to swim away on the surface when a larger crocodile clamped down on him and pulled him under the water, where he would drown. And toward this chaotic scene Ndovu's mother and the herd led the young elephant.

The river was now thirty-two miles away and the elephants were starting to return to their original herds. Ironically, some lions who drank from the river now moved back and lay in wait for the antelopes who, like the elephants, were heading toward the river. The lions had been safe through the drought because the blood of their prey provided them with moisture. Still, water is preferred and the lions in the area came in to drink, and then went out to hunt. Sometimes, however, they added to the crocodile carnage at the river's edge and hunted there. Leopards dropped from trees, seizing animals who had come far and suffered long. Hyenas cackled and circled the scene night and day.

No animal was thirsty once the river was reached, and no animal was hungry. Those who ate grass were readily supplied; those who wanted leaves found all they needed in the moist river valley, giraffes feeding on high branches and gerenuks feeding on the lower ones. Predators had ten thousand times their immediate needs, rarely more than a lunge away. There was carnage, but also satiation; there was survival and the system remained intact. And Ndovu arrived at the river.

4

THE RIVER AND THE MARSH

Ndovu learned the most important lesson of his life on the long walk to the river. Simply, it was that for the elephant water is everything. Its size dictates the amount of water an elephant needs, as well as the quantity of fresh green food that only water can sustain.

It is believed that there may be rare but essential trace elements that are found only in small amounts in the plants that the elephant consumes. If the animal digested all of the leaves and grass that it ate, it might get too little of the rare things it requires to run so large a machine. By digesting only half of its harvest, it is able to eat twice as much and therefore get a sufficient amount of these yet unidentified nutrients. That may be why elephants can smell water, which sustains all plant life, a hundred miles away and maybe even farther than that.

The pace of the herd increased as the smell of water became more intense. The feeding frenzy of the crocodiles registered with the elephants, and they carried their ears outspread to hear the finer details of sound. Almost everything that was happening at the river came to them by scent or sound. They were alert, yet desperate to not only get to the water but into it. It had been over a week since they had been able to soak and spray water and mud over their backs, and both the sun and swarms of insects had been harsh to them.

A few miles from the river, individuals in the herd had come close to the end of their endurance. A number had suffered from heatstroke. They had become lethargic, shuffling along more like robots than living animals. They appeared depressed and reacted badly, almost as if shocked by any sudden sounds or movement. However, their social structure was a major source of strength that kept them going. If they had had to make the journey alone, few would have survived. The sounds and smells of familiar companions and their frequent touch kept them together and literally kept them alive. When an elephant lays its trunk across the withers of another, it is the greatest medicine for treating and sustaining these giants. Without it, a strange and little understood disease known as Seyle's Syndrome can set in, and elephants may simply lie down and die. The disease is often referred to as a "broken heart," because these giants of the earth seem to sometimes simply give up on life, and "decide" they want to die.

As the smell of water intensified even more, the herd's pace increased. A hundred yards before they reached the top of the last slope above the river, several of the elephants shrilled loud blasts and then grumbled in a deep growl. Any hoofed stock or predators who had been unaware of the approaching animals from the ground vibrations knew then that it was time to move away. Once the elephants topped the ridge, nothing on earth would stop them. The river's odor had grown stronger with every mile, and they were nearly in a frenzy. The sun burned brightly in the sky behind them, turning them into huge silhouettes. Against that vivid yellow scrim they hovered for just a moment, and then poured down the slope toward the water.

Careful of their footing, the giants cascaded down into the river. Even the crocodiles pulled back. They were sated anyway and did not need food, would not need it for months. Even if they had been hungry, however, they would not attack the adult elephants, nor even the young if the adults were at hand. About a mile upstream from where Ndovu and his mother reached the water, a crocodile had not pulled away quite fast enough. A bull impaled him on one tusk, and then used his foot to dislodge him and toss his body aside.

The elephants waded out into the river until the tallest of the bulls were almost totally submerged. The cows with young sat down on their haunches nearer to the bank, then rolled over onto their sides, keeping the tips of their trunks just above water. Later they stood and sprayed the now thoroughly muddied water over their backs, and drank great quantities, filling their trunks and blowing the water into their mouths. The tips of the coiled trunks rested on their bottom lips, which they rolled into gutters to receive the bounty. Rivulets of water ran out of the corners of their mouths and it seemed as if they would never get enough. Beyond actual thirst, there was the sheer joy of not being thirsty and of being wet.

Along the banks where the elephants waded, the water was now opaque from mud and animal droppings. The churning stretched for three miles along the river's edge, and fish and other aquatic life left for less crowded areas. Because of their size, elephants are rowdies at water holes and in rivers. They wade and shuffle, roll, scuffle, and spray thousands of gallons, creating a mist that splits the rays of the sun into a million prisms, forming many rainbows.

As well-mannered as they normally are, when they intrude upon a system as finely tuned and fragile as a watercourse, elephants cause mayhem. But they are seldom as happy, as thoroughly contented, as when engaging in a great community swimfest and water frolic. When sated, they stand apart from each other, frequently up to their bellies in water and mud, and contemplate whatever comes to an elephant's mind when all stress has drained away. Elephants in water and full of water are at peace and retreat to their inner selves.

The pressure of more elephants arriving on the slope pushed those already there across the river to the far bank. Ndovu's mother led him through shallow water to a partially submerged riverine island. By moving to the upstream end of the island, they avoided the deeper channels. While the infant was in the water, Ndovu's mother kept her trunk coiled around his belly and at one point even supported him with his feet off solid ground. Soon both banks of the river were crowded with elephants. Animals who had had their fill began to drift back, making way for the rest of the herd. The land predators stayed away, preferring to avoid the elephants, particularly those with young. Marabou storks stood like huge shrouded judges on the riverine islands along the banks and in the tops of trees. They looked somber and disapproving. Although they are storks, they live like vultures, and like all carrion eaters, they are opportunistic and very serious about their task.

Early on the previous day a high-altitude wind had shifted toward the west, gathering moisture over the Indian Ocean and carrying it toward the continent. It was nudged onto its course by huge sandstorms blowing across the eastern reaches of the Sahara and down the mountain ridges of Ethiopia. A low-pressure area had formed over the Great Rift Valley and with the arrival of the moisture-laden clouds, the air fairly dripped with the humidity. By early afternoon on the day of Ndovu's arrival at the river, the sky had begun to darken far earlier than usual. By four o'clock, thunder could be heard; then it was overhead.

Streaks of lightning shot down and surged into trees, shattering some to splinters. Small fires started in a dozen places, including along the riverbanks where the elephants were resting, but none really caught on. Rain was sweeping across the land in sheets, quenching every spark. The surface of the river was pocked, then masked entirely, as the rain came into it almost horizontally, sweeping back and forth with the fickle winds. Out in the middle of the channel, crocodiles floated like a congregation of submerged trees and became almost invisible. The world turned quickly from earth tones of umber and gold to the silver and blue-gray of the deluge.

Animals that less than twenty-four hours before had been near death from dehydration now stood near torrents of water. The river boiled coming down the course, for the storm stretched over fifty miles upstream. Riverbanks disappeared, nearby low areas became marshes, and amphibians moved from their moist hiding places by the thousands, only to be crushed by tens of thousands of hoofs as the herds milled around uneasily. Ironically, the downpour would have done little for the animals had they not reached the valley of the river. The storm did not extend out to the areas stricken with drought, the areas from which the herds had come. Much of the water would reach other drought areas downstream, however, as the river surged southward, then fanned out into a giant marsh, scores of miles across.

No one knows when the very small animals die; a toad or a frog, for example, vanishes unheralded. But on this night an elephant died. In the worst of the electric crescendos a bolt of lightning struck Ndovu's elder sister, one of the cows who had stood guard at his birth. She was standing just slightly apart from her aunt in the middle of their herd when a finger of electric fire singled her out. For just a minute she seemed to glow, and then the huge quantity of gas in her guts exploded, opening a jagged slit along the midline of her belly, as if there had been a zipper there. Her brain boiled at the moment of the lightning's impact, so she felt no pain. One mo-

A lizard perches on a high rock out of the way of larger animals during a flash flood. ❖

ment she was, and the next moment she was not. She lay on her side with her intestines spilling out onto the ground. The elephants near her moaned and keened and a few came to inspect her and to urge her with prodding tusks and inquiring trunks to stand again, to undo the moment just past. But the young cow remained still.

Ndovu would not remember his sister. His world still consisted entirely of one other animal, his mother.

The storm passed down the river, moving south, and by the time midnight had come everything was quiet. Young elephants, many, like Ndovu, having just experienced their first real storm, stood close to their mothers while the other members of the herd stood facing one another, somewhat subdued. Now only the timid sounds of the amphibians throbbed. The occasional *kaah-kah-kah-kaaah* cackle of a zebra and the low moaning of wildebeest cows seeking their young told what was out in the darkness beyond the elephants and the river.

Sunrise found mist rising off the swollen river and from the marsh nearby. The animals, the many thousands of them, glowed yellow and gold as the sun sent slanting rays through the newly cleansed sky. Ndovu and his mother and all the elephants around them shimmered, for they were still wet. It was as if a translucent layer of gold paint had been washed across black bark.

Slowly, one by one, the elephants spread out and began to feed. In the lingering mists of the morning they called to one another in friendly, unchallenging trumpets and moans, and only occasionally in sounds more

Elephants stand peacefully in a river swollen after a thunderstorm. ❖

shrill. They were content. They had made the great trek and only a few had died.

❖ ❖ ❖

The morning after the storm found the herd a mile from the river in the renewed marsh. In every direction elephants had spread out, standing in water. Some were belly deep or more, others stood with water at or below their knees. The lush vegetation was mush-soft and sweet, unlike the harsh, dry fare they had relied upon during their journey to the river. It was a giant buffet and there was more than enough of it, even for elephants. Trunks prodded and probed and tore off whatever appealed most at the moment. Small fish picked at their leavings, and egrets and jacanas, gallinules and crakes stood in the shallows or walked across the pads of plants that rose from submerged roots, and had their leaves now facing the sun. Pigmy geese, coots, teal, pochards, and ducks swam among the giants in small, well-ordered flotillas, and marsh harriers moved back and forth. Fish eagles called in their strangely small, scratchy voices while plovers—spur-winged, blacksmith, and Kittlitz—moved along the banks. Stilts flew in to join the pulse of the marsh, and some avocets appeared. Water snakes swam their sinuous courses, and there was relative calm. Small hunters, out of sight but no less deadly for their size, hunted their small prey, but among the larger animals it was a time of peace.

Ndovu waggled after his mother as she moved along the edge of the marsh, keeping to solid ground. His tail swished and his still quite useless trunk hung loose, flopping aimlessly, and his ears flapped as well. All of his parts would eventually come under his control, but for the present he was more like a soft toy than a king of the African land.

When the cow found a place that seemed solid enough to support her infant son, she turned toward the marsh and waded in to ankle depth. Suddenly she stopped, snapped her ears out and forward, and took a step backward, her tail out almost as straight as her trunk. Then she blasted a single shrill warning note that galvanized Ndovu. Across the marsh other elephants stopped harvesting just long enough to see if there would be another, more informative note. None came, and they went back to their feeding.

From the reeds just ahead of the cow, a beast as prehistoric as her own kind rose up and faced her, head low, two long horns menacing. As if in a scene from the Pleistocene Age, a black, or more properly, a *prehensile-lipped,* rhinoceros stood facing her. He had been taking his ease in the marsh, for he too needed the protection of mud against biting insects. A peaceful harvester of vegetation like the elephants, he was, however, wary of intruders. The cow elephant and bull rhinoceros had startled each other, and animals, large as well as small, dislike surprises. A really large elephant can weigh six and a half tons, thirteen thousand pounds, while a large rhinoceros will seldom weigh much more than three thousand pounds. Still, there is a kind of mutual respect, for neither animal intrudes upon the other nor eats the flesh of other animals. And certainly, in and around the marsh there was food and water enough for all.

Although he would never have reason to fear, much less fight, a rhinoceros, Ndovu would remain suspicious of them as long as he lived. No amount of experience

A black rhinoceros presents a menacing appearance, but like the elephant, eats only plants. ❖

would enable him to erase or override the signals his mother had given when she found the rhinoceros almost under her feet. She had taught her calf to react defensively to surprises, a worthwhile lesson, but she had also inadvertently taught him to distrust a species that was harmless to him. It is an illustration of how individual animals, even when surrounded by a herd, can develop their own unique reactions.

The rhinoceros pushed himself up out of the muck at the first sound from Ndovu's mother and moved off, keeping parallel with the edge of the swamp, his tail held high, his enormous front horn probing on ahead. He was soon lost in the tall reeds. Ndovu and his mother moved down into shallow water where she fed, and he continued his exploration of the sensations of water, mud, and soft plants. She kept him close to her, and soon they glistened black as she showered them both with water.

Farther out, near the center of the marsh, there was a large pond. It had the deepest water around, and in it about two dozen giants of a third species of animal sank and rose, making great blowing noises and echoing deep *unkch-unkch-unkch* sounds in a challenging way. Hippopotamuses, weighing as much as six thousand pounds, are the most combative of the three giant species. What is often taken as a hippo's "yawn" is really a threat display, warning lesser males away from an area known as the crèche, where breedable females assemble with their young. Anything from a man in a boat to a crocodile that floats into a territory adjacent to the local crèche, may find itself crushed in massive jaws. But hippos and elephants don't battle one another either, so the sounds,

Hippopotamuses spend much time in the water. Easily aroused, they can be dangerous to smaller animals, including man. ❖

while mildly interesting to Ndovu, elicited no response from his mother and none from him.

Every hour of every day was learning time for Ndovu, and everything he encountered became an educational toy. He would seek the sheer luxury, the endless comfort of marshes all of his days, and now was his time to explore them.

The herd remained in and near the marsh for three days, and then for reasons only elephants know, they moved off toward the south. Why elephants struggle so hard to find water, only to leave it after a short time, is a mystery. There are at least two possible explanations: They are so destructive to an area that nature has had to program them to keep moving to conserve habitat, or perhaps they need nutrients not found near water and know in their way that they must seek it elsewhere. On the fourth day after the storm, the herd came over a ridge twelve miles from the river and moved down in single file, except for Ndovu and the other young, who remained at their mothers' sides.

5

THE FUNERAL

Forty miles west of the great basin, the herd came to a second range of hills, purple in the distance, but green, brown, and gold as they came closer. They climbed to the crest of a middle-sized hill, paused briefly to test the air, and then  they started the descent toward the valley floor. Elephants prefer using known trails to breaking new ground, and their paths may have been in use for millennia. Some trails in geologically stable areas were in use long, long before present species of animals evolved. African elephants now walk in the petrified footprints of ancient dinosaurs.

Somehow elephants appear to understand the peril of their own size. A fall on a hillside and rocks that can be dislodged are things elephants cannot afford to risk. They will go out of their way to avoid hazardous footing. Each animal knows that food and water must be located within a certain time, to ensure its survival. Because of its enormous weight, an elephant that falls risks a broken bone. This could slow up the whole herd and endanger the lives of the other animals. The herd can wait only a short time to accommodate an individual. Then it must move on.

Under normal circumstances the giants move slowly and in an orderly fashion. A female almost always leads the herd when it is on the move. She is usually old and very wise and the others depend on her for guidance. She is alert to anything new, anything out of place on the wind or in the sound waves that she monitors constantly. Elephants do have amazing memories and once they have passed a place, they know it; they know what if anything has changed since their last passage, and that the matriarch will tell them if it matters. Elephants are not afraid for their own safety—they never had to be until man and his greed for trophies and ivory appeared—but they are afraid for their young. They worry about disorder too. Time, trees, grass, brush, termite hills, natural landforms, water, mates, the other species they expect to encounter, and the few with which they interact at all, all have their places. Elephants don't like to be disturbed, and disorder disturbs them as much as anything can. What may appear as chaos to observers who see trees being pulled down actually is part of a very orderly system. Elephants evolved on a continent where there were so many trees that even destruction on a massive scale scarcely mattered. If the herd turned a wooded area into a nearly treeless savannah, it didn't matter. They didn't have to pass that place again until a new woodland had appeared. There

An elephant herd is usually led by an older female. With her extraordinary senses of smell and hearing, she will alert the herd to any danger. ❖

were plenty of trees when elephants first evolved, and the change from that abundance has caught them up short. Today's elephants live in a time of dreadful reckoning.

As the herd descended the far side of the hill, still in single file, the lead cow began showing signs of agitation. Her alarm ran back through her followers like an electric current. Then suddenly she stopped in her tracks, forcing the rest to hold themselves in position behind her. Those in the rear turned and faced backward, their trunks and ears outstretched, automatically assuming the role of rear guard. Until the cause of the matriarch's concern was known, they would act as if they were being besieged. A low rumbling swept back through the herd, rolling over and over from animal to animal like distant thunder. Ndovu and the other infants felt the tension and moved closer to their mothers.

The lead cow snapped her ears forward several times, then moved her trunk back and forth. Her deep grumbling was punctuated with shrill blasts. Two diminutive dik-diks, antelopes not very much larger than rabbits, fighting in a territorial dispute just ahead of the herd, parted, then fled. A small herd of male impalas, a so-called bachelor herd, made incredibly graceful ballet leaps and vanished. A leopard lying among hillside rocks, less than a quarter of a mile away, decamped and dissolved behind a huge boulder. Still the lead cow trumpeted, and the others behind her joined in a deafening chorus. The old matriarch swayed, flapped her ears in growing consternation, and reached for further evidence as her trunk continued to explore on ahead. She took several steps to her right, then to her left, and at last, having fixed the cause of the trouble, suddenly moved ahead at a very fast walk. On the flat, open ground where the slope leveled off lay a heap of bones too large to be anything but the remains of an elephant. The round mound formed by the animal's empty rib cage seemed to grin at the sky through what appeared to be widespread teeth of enormous length. The skull was still attached to the vertebrae. Most of the animal's structure, in fact, was made of bones too large to be moved very far by any of the many scavengers that had come to feed. The matriarch and her followers circled the skeleton, their initial shrieks having turned now to shrill keening and moaning.

No one knows how elephants identify the skeletal remains of one of their own kind, but they do. The smell of an elephant dead for several weeks is unique. Elephants ignore the thousands of other bone piles they pass in their wanderings, but they know their own. They know long before their poor eyesight can distinguish a thigh bone from a termite hill, long before they are close enough to recognize anything by sight. Still, they seem to know. And they don't like to encounter their own kind that way.

As they circled the giant skeleton, the elephants moved in closer. At first Ndovu's mother held back and circled, seemingly aimlessly, about thirty feet away. Other cows with infant calves did the same thing. But Ndovu and his mother soon joined the main herd. Ndovu did not know how to keen and moan like the adults, but the mood, whatever it was, had gripped him too, and he expressed his own tension by blowing air through his trunk, occasionally producing a squeaking sound. He did not know what was happening, but it was an ancient rite and he participated as well as he could. Young though he was, he was becoming an integral part of the herd.

Then the matriarch stopped, moved into the bone pile, and kicked it with her right forefoot, dislodging a leg bone. She wrapped her trunk around it and pulled it free. She held it high in front of her, and with her tail straight out and ears extended, she marched toward a grove of trees a hundred yards away. Breaking through the screen of brush and scattering two duikers, small antelopes, that were hiding there, she put the heavy bone down. Then she began tearing down branches and putting them on top of the bone. Soon it was covered. She wheeled around and went back to the bone pile that was now rapidly diminishing as the other members of the herd followed her example. Within forty-five minutes of its discovery the bone pile had vanished, and the individual pieces, from ribs to pelvis, were buried over an area of several hundred acres. In all cases vegetation, not dirt, formed their cover. Only the dead animal's skull remained, and the matriarch, alone at first but then with the help of two other cows, edged it along toward the woodland, using their partially coiled trunks and their tusks. Finally it too was covered with uprooted and dislodged branches. It is doubtful that the elephants noticed that there were no tusks for them to carry away and cover. If the animal had died a natural death, there would have been. The bull who died there, however, had been thirty-four years old. He had been a robust

The matriarch of a herd is the first to explore unfamiliar or suspicious areas. ❖

animal and could have lived another thirty to thirty-five years.

Should the herd ever pass that way again, its members would remember the dead bull and cast around, seek clues that were now back with the earth. By that time the cobra who had hidden briefly in the skull of the elephant would have fed a secretary bird's nestling young after dying a violent death. Africa, as it always does, folds over events, lets them play out, but ultimately absorbs them and brings some kind of order back out of chaos. It is like a never-ending theatrical drama. The players come and go, play their parts, speak their lines, and then they are replaced as the new scenario begins.

6

SODA LAKE

Ndovu went through the stages of his growth as his herd moved through the ever-changing areas where the major events of his life occurred. There had been the great grass fire and the terror it had caused; the long, agonizing  journey in the search for water; then the river and the marsh; the crocodile massacre; and masses of so many species; the place of the dead bull and the mourning there. After each episode Ndovu was subtly changed. He learned constantly, each event teaching him how to be an elephant. Much of what he knew was instinctive, but he needed to learn more in order to survive. He needed experience too. What were passing events for the adults in his herd were important stages in the growth and development of the young bull.

At the age of three Ndovu had at last been weaned. He had been sampling vegetation for almost a year by then, but still relied on his mother's milk for much of his food until she began refusing to let him nurse. Finally she had stopped producing milk. Now he would learn from his mother, and other herd members, everything he needed to know about the thousands of plants he would encounter.

The herd now numbered between fifty and seventy animals. Bulls came and went, seeking breeding opportunities or perhaps brief periods of companionship. The younger bulls, the teenagers, who were so full of themselves that they were a nuisance to the adults and possibly a danger to the very young, were not tolerated and were driven off. All such decisions were made by the older cows. They ruled. One day Ndovu too would be expelled.

The herd grew too. For although pregnancy is long in elephants, births are regular events.

Ndovu would eventually learn to eat sixty-five different kinds of plants. From some he would take fruit, from others leaves. Some would provide bark, a few even pulpy wood, and from still others, mineral-laden roots rich in nutrition but hard on an animal's teeth. He would harvest his fodder in huge quantities, for he was destined to be huge himself.

During his life Ndovu would develop seven molarlike teeth in each half of his upper and lower jaws. He would never have more than two teeth in each half of each jaw, working and wearing away, largely eroded by the sand that came in with clumps of grass. As the front tooth of the pair was worn down, the tooth behind it would complete its development and migrate forward. When that no longer happens, when new teeth no longer come forward, an elephant weakens and dies. The normal allotment is six deciduous, or shedding, teeth on each side of both jaws. A few elephants get a seventh tooth, but it isn't common.

At three Ndovu weighed almost fourteen hundred pounds. Stubby tusks had erupted on each side of his upper jaw, and they would continue to grow for most of his life. Eventually they would have a combined weight of 238 pounds, large tusks by any standard, far larger than is found in most elephants. The great beasts are routinely slaughtered for their ivory long before their tusks reach that size.

When fully grown, Ndovu would weigh eleven thousand pounds and stand over thirteen and a half feet tall at the shoulder. That would all happen in the first forty years of his life. He would eventually exhibit all the signs of elephant beauty: The bases of his tail and trunk would be broad, his skin would be very wrinkled, his legs would be heavy, his body well-balanced and square. His ears would be huge and would perform many roles. They would increase his apparent size and would drive off insects. They would gather sound to an incredible degree, and fully supplied with blood vessels, they would help him regulate his body temperature much the way that a car's radiator works for an engine. They would help him communicate, and express his moods. Other animals would watch his ears and know how he felt. He was calm or very dangerous. Ndovu would be an elephant to be reckoned with.

Young though he was and as unimpressive as his new tusks were, Ndovu was already trying both them and

The elephant's huge ears help him to have very acute hearing by directing sounds inward, and also aid in regulating his body temperature. ❖

himself. He would stand face to face with other males of his age, and they would push against one another. Their trunks, now under their control and no longer just floppy fingerlike projections, would be raised and intertwined as the youngsters leaned into each other and prodded each other with their stubby tusks. They pushed with their hind legs, extended them out to the rear, and it was not uncommon for them to slip and slide and go to their knees, sometimes even over onto their sides. A year earlier they had climbed and crawled over each other in their games like enormous puppies, but that was too dangerous now. They had become too heavy and had evolved new strategies for play and other interactions. The testing, though, would go on for years, and from it a pecking order would emerge. When it got too rough, an adult in the herd would issue a warning and the young bulls would back off. When they failed to respond, they would be sent away to find a lone bull and travel with him as his askaris, or guards.

For the time being, though, Ndovu was safe in the herd and attentive to the guidance and the warnings. He still had to learn the manners demanded by the cows. The older he got, the less tolerant they would become of him and his aggressive behavior. He was surrounded by tenderness, for elephants are tender animals, but it was authoritative too. For elephants, especially cows, are authoritative animals.

During his lifetime Ndovu would never wander more than two hundred and fifty miles from the equator. He would cross the line on numerous occasions and wander into very low northern latitudes, but generally he would stay south of the earth's waistline. He would never venture to grounds lower than five thousand feet above sea level, and only rarely would he go as high as ten thousand feet. He would seldom be out of the shadow of the highest freestanding mountain in the world, Mount Kilimanjaro. At 19,340 feet that single mountain has one fifth of all the ice on the African continent ringing its crown. Its high, flat-topped peak called Mawenzi is hidden in cumulus clouds much of the time. A higher, pointed peak, Kibo, is more often seen but is also often lost in the sky. The two peaks are thought to be a single mountain, one of the best known in the world.

Because he would wander so close to the equator all of his life and in such a narrow band of altitudes, Ndovu would never know the four seasons common to most of the earth. Summer, winter, fall, and spring belonged to other worlds. In Ndovu's world there were only dry and wet times. During the latter periods he would tend to stay in one place. During dry spells he would journey as his herd had done when he was an infant, searching for places where water was still falling or at least where it had not yet evaporated.

As the herd moved away from the river and marsh, it passed through a strange forest where the trees looked like giant candelabra and many pythons hunted. In time the herd came upon new vegetation surrounding a large body of water that was so hot and bitter with chemicals, it was of no use to the elephants. The animals strung out in single file as they approached the lake through a great stand of yellow fever trees. The leading animals stopped where the trees ended and the following animals came up alongside of them until a line of elephants stretched for nearly a mile. They were barely hidden by shrubbery and the scene they looked upon was strange and confusing to the young animals. Typically their eyes registered little of what lay before them, but their other senses alerted them to the phenomenon.

The sound coming from the lake was overwhelming. There were periodic whooshing noises when underground geothermal springs erupted through steaming, chemical-stained cones in the form of geysers. Nearly two million flamingos, stately but rather startling in their garish pink finery, were at the lake, and a quarter of a million pelicans as well. The din of the chattering birds, the sound of the escaping steam, and the cascading water combined to create an atmosphere seemingly not of this planet.

The flat, open area around the lake reeked, layered deep in flamingo dung, for this was a traditional flamingo lake in use for thousands of years. Rafts of the brilliantly colored birds lifted away periodically, their legs trailing behind them, and flew in layers, frequently moving in opposite directions. The birds were slashes of otherworldly color, standing out sharply against the black and purple hills that completely enclosed the basin. Hundreds of white pelicans were frequently aloft at the same time, wheeling above the flamingos. Overhead, eagles and vultures soared as they will wherever the massing of animals becomes profoundly large. The steam from the geysers and the lake water was like ghostly gray fingers against the dark background, seeming to point toward the birds in the sky.

Ndovu stood between his mother and another cow and looked out toward the lake. He could distinguish no more with his eyes than his herd mates, but the sounds

Although elephants, like most animals, can't tolerate the strong alkalinity of a soda lake, flamingos and some other birds are unaffected by it. ❖

and smells were unmistakable. Hyenas by the dozens stalked back and forth around the edges of the lake, frequently going hock-deep in the flamingo dung, pulling their legs free with a sucking, popping sound. Each such penetration seemed to release even more noxious gas into the air that hung heavy over the water and the surrounding land. Waterbucks, impalas, dozens of warthogs with babies scurrying behind moved through the short grass just back from the edge of the dung. The temperature was twenty degrees higher near the lake than it was at the edge of the trees and Ndovu felt the beginning of the rise in heat as soon as he had taken the first few steps out onto the flat. He pressed hard against his mother's hip as they fell in line. It was a strange new world where nothing was familiar. The blurred pink clouds, the sudden rise in temperature, the cacophony of sound, the stench—it was frightening to come upon for the first time. Signals poured into his sensory net at the rate of thousands of data bits per second. He tried to sort them out, and was only partially successful.

Before all of the elephants had come out of the forest, there was a sudden explosion of sound, a mixture of rage and alarm. A leopard had foolishly dropped from a heavy tree limb near where a cow and a very young calf were passing. The cat probably didn't intend to try for the calf, but the rage he encountered was immediate and unrelenting. The leopard arched his back, twisted into a half circle, and tried to back away. But before he could escape, three other elephants were upon him, bursting through the brush that grew below the trees. In less than a minute he was flattened, dismembered, trod upon, and gored. However inadvertently he had approached a herd of elephants with newborn young, there is no more dangerous encounter on earth, for in such moments every cow is the mother of every calf, and every bull their defender.

At the first cry of rage by the calf's mother, the flamingos had flown away. Now they returned by the hundreds of thousands, dropping back into their soda-rich soup of a lake. The pelicans too, in the tens of thousands, were wheeling overhead, ready for their descent as well. The sun inched down behind the western rim, and it was night when the herd reached a cut in the land that led into the forest beyond the basin, up through the hills, and onto a high and fertile plateau beyond.

7

THE PLATEAU

The herd made the long, steep climb up from the soda lake through the V-shaped cut in the hills. It was nightfall when they reached a sweet, fast-flowing stream that led back into the forest. The soda lake had offered them noth-  ing, and they wanted to get away from its noise and heat and sour smell. The elephants passed from the subdued light of the day's end to near total black- ness as they en- tered the forest. There was only the merest sliver of a moon and none of its feeble light could push down through the thick canopy. In such places as this, scent and sound are more important than visual signals.

The herd moved, scores of tons of elephants, with less noise than the sound of the flamingos' wings against the air. It is an astonishing fact that the elephant's movement is virtually soundless, even in dense brush.

Its passage is usually masked by the sounds of insects.

For a hundred yards the herd followed the stream-bed, wading in the cool, clear water that cascaded down from the plateau above. Below, it would be fouled by soda and dung once it reached the edge of the flamingo lake. Small animals by the hundreds pulled back as the herd paddled through the water, ascending slowly up the hill from which it came. Duikers, impalas, dik-diks, lions, and dozens of other species backed off as the elephants approached. Diminutive bush babies bounced between the trees like tennis balls and then vanished into the branches above, somehow able to ignore the needle-sharp thorns that could flay a man alive. Tree hyraxes, rabbit-sized animals that are believed to be the elephants' nearest kin, rattled their evening calls, sounding more like machinery than animals. An excessively shy and characteristically solitary bongo, displaying magnificent horns, dissolved between the trees, ghostlike in his shyness, magical in his ability to make it seem as if he had never been there at all. A little farther on there were other ghosts, several equally retiring lesser kudus pulled back too. Overhead, monkeys slept, and only when a python slithered out onto a branch did any of them react to the night. One monkey died, dozens screamed in protest, but they were soon asleep again and the young python withdrew. A caracal had moved down from the savannah above and took an African hare that had been cowering under a bush. A spotted genet cat, not a cat at all but a relative of the mongoose, took a rabbit. A five-foot-long monitor lizard fed on ground-nesting birds' eggs.

The elephants heard every sound whispered in the

secret forest places, smelled each creature in the vicinity, but reacted only to two male lions lying in a clearing near a recent kill. A rumbling started along the line and several cows and a partially grown bull shrilled terrifying warning blasts. For a moment the forest was full of noise, but then the chorus subsided into lesser cries and a hush came down. Ndovu listened carefully to the orchestration of sounds, for there were signals that were important for him to know. He would eventually learn to read the night by all its sounds and smells.

The lions understood the elephants' message and were soon well away, grumbling to themselves. They were full of zebra meat and didn't want to leave their kill. Much of the animal remained uneaten and could have served the cats well a dozen hours later. Now other animals would certainly claim it, and the cats would have to kill again the next day. Lions kill no more often than they have to, for there is danger in hunting and exertion as well. Cats of all kinds prefer to store kinetic energy rather than expend it.

Once safely away the great cats lowered their heads until their chins were barely off the ground. They hunched up their bodies for a mightly push and used the very earth itself as a sounding chamber as they roared their defiance. Once again the quiet was broken, but it soon returned and covered the evening again like a blanket. The elephants heard the lions, of course, and were satisfied. The quality of the sound told them the cats were safely out of their way. All animals understand display and bravado; it can be measured, it can be judged. And

Lions may be known as kings of the jungle, but they readily give way to the much more powerful elephants, the true kings. ❖

many species require it of each other in order to establish dominance and territorial rights.

Eventually the stream became a waterfall, and the elephants turned and passed along the base of the escarpment. The plunging stream broke over them as they plodded through it. Ndovu hesitated for just a moment before pushing on through the wall of the cascade, but his mother had moved on ahead and he was quick enough to follow. Once he had taken the first terrifying step and the water was hissing around him, he began to enjoy the sensation and slowed down to sense it, for it was new. As with everything he now encountered, he studied it, experienced it, decided for himself if it was good. A cow pushing from the rear and his mother calling from on ahead made him pick up his pace and push on.

The stench and sounds of the flamingo lake were well behind the elephants now, and the forest smelled clean and fresh. The mold and the fungi were sweet, the humus and the new growth as well. The herd emerged from under the waterfall to an area of loose rock shale. It appeared as a series of flat tables of black rock, one only an inch or two higher or lower than another. Water had gathered in depressions filled by small side streams. The elephants spread out to drink from the clear pools and to linger briefly and rest from their climb up the streambed beneath the tall trees. They pulled vegetation down from the branches overhead and stripped bushes of their youngest growth. The rocks were slippery, and the adults in the herd moved carefully, probing with their trunks, avoiding edges where the hill fell away. The more adventurous of the young were less cautious, and the shale area reverberated with warning sounds as cows called them back from the edges where the footing was less certain. The infants responded quickly, but one young bull, particularly active and already showing aggressive behavior, did not react quickly enough. His mother's signal was plain, but at four-and-half years old (a "teenager" in elephant terms) he was dangerously full of himself. He backed away shaking his head from side to side, flapping his already impressive ears and flopping his trunk. Finally the young bull stepped back too far and felt his left hind foot begin to slip off the edge. He reacted to the threat quickly, struggled, but he went to his knees and began to roll. He couldn't stop himself. He went over into the hollow night below with a shrill blast of terror. His mother came forward but stayed back from the edge, held in check by her own native caution. She blasted and keened as she heard her calf crash down through the trees and land on another table of flat shale forty-six feet below. Ndovu could hear the moaning, and pushed hard against his mother. The other herd members moved back and forth, crowding each other, worrying together, for among elephants worrying is a communal activity, but there was nothing that they could do even if they had fully understood what had happened.

The herd couldn't reach the young bull. Several tried going back under the fall and down the streambed for a hundred yards, but there was no way through. The shale between the streambed and the lower table where the young bull had landed had collapsed and was disintegrating. There was no possible footing for an elephant. It might have been adequate for baboons, snakes, and the least of the antelopes, but rockfalls and avalanches are too dangerous for elephants to suffer and survive. Their own weight works against them, and a fall of any kind is likely to be deadly.

The moaning and the pleading calls to the young bull's mother were monitored by the whole herd and it stayed on the high flat shale formation for hours after the terrible sounds had stopped. Not until well after the young bull had died from his injuries did the lead cow turn away and head up the diagonal path that finally led to the plateau. Ndovu did not understand what had happened, but it had been bad and all of the signals reinforced the sense of terror and sorrow that now swept through the herd. Ndovu, because he could not understand the sequence of events that had occurred, couldn't learn from it. One lesson he already knew: Stay close to the adults, do what they do, listen to their calls and signals, for in every sense those calls are advice.

The young bull's mother was the last animal to fall in line as the herd moved off, but eventually, however reluctantly, she did so too. Periodically she stopped and turned as if waiting for her son to catch up, to come rushing to her side. He never did, never would. She would still be looking for him a week later, although by then her remarkable memory would have begun to fade and she would gradually become more attentive to the other calves in the herd. Her broodiness would be spent on them, and she would be nurturing to even largely grown animals. She would have to spend what her glands had programmed inside of her, as part of a sequence that had started with conception six and a half years earlier. She could not just cast it all away. The death of her son had removed the focus but not the need for caring.

As dawn came in across the hills, the lead cow and the animals immediately behind her pushed out of the trees, through the lower bushes, and emerged onto a flat plateau. It was cut here and there by streams that reached for the edges of the high plain and then cascaded off into space. Spread out before the herd was a giant congregation of hoofed animals. Over a hundred thousand wildebeests bleated and grunted their strange unmusical sounds.

Over thirty thousand common zebras, with their broad stripes running full around their bellies, grazed in groups from two to twenty. Many of their young were lying on the ground, and most of the mares without newly born young seemed about to give birth. The stallions also had distended bellies, but internal parasites had caused them. Strikingly built roan, kongoni, and topi, large antelopes with sloping backs, wandered in the midst of the herds, worrying about the predators that hung back at a distance. There were four adult cheetahs, all solitary except for a female with three half-grown cubs. A pride of seven lions slept off their last feast less than a mile away.

A single, round-faced leopard sprawled on a tree limb on the far side of the plain. That night he would make a kill by dropping off his tree limb almost on top of a lone male impala. It would be quick and easy. The grass was deep in some areas and lynxlike caracals and spotted serval cats looked for opportunities to take young gazelles. Hyenas were everywhere watching, waiting,

Cape buffalos are among the many hoofed animals that live on the plains of equatorial Africa. ❖

willing to steal the carcasses of the victims of other predators, but equally willing to kill for themselves. There were scores of them in and out of deep burrows. They drooled and they cackled, they watched and they waited. They would all eat soon enough.

There were four species of gazelles—the Thomson, Grant, impala, and the incredibly graceful gerenuks, which stood on their hind legs to feed high after the fashion of the very much taller giraffes. On the far side of the plateau another trail led down a thousand feet below. There tall trees grew for about a thousand yards, and seventeen Masai giraffes fed on the topmost branches. Although hidden deep in their burrows, several piglike aardvarks waited for the night, while warthogs scampered along, usually a mother with her young. They kept their tails erect so that they could spot each other when the grass was deep, and get together again if it became necessary to scatter. In the trees that ringed the plateau, the bush babies were curled into balls, sleeping away the day that was now full upon the high plain, as the last of the elephants moved up the final yards of the trail. They left behind the forested slope and moved out onto the grassy flatland with its ample supply of water. Owls, too, waited in trees nearby. It was day and the shift was completed. Nocturnal animals were well hidden, others who hunted at dawn and dusk were quitting the stage and the diurnal animals were as active as circumstances allowed. They would all try to feed and drink before the sun was high and the heat of the day was upon them.

Three species of eagles soared over the area and then perched in the trees at its edge. There were two tawny

Giraffes feed on the high branches of tall trees on the Masai plains. ❖

eagles, three bateleurs, and several long-crested eagles too. In the course of the day two martial eagles, a lone African hawk eagle, and a half a dozen species of hawks, falcons, and buzzards would rise on the thermals that came up from below as the temperature rose. The smaller mammals would watch for shadows and remain on worried alert. Everything that lived on the plateau would try not to die that day, but millions—including insects and arthropods—would fail and would reenter the system that had spawned them. Some larger players would finish their journeys there that day as well.

Huge koribustards stalked the grass with absurd dignity and self-importance, looking for lizards and large insects. Black and red ground hornbills did the same, ungainly and turkeylike as they waddled after anything that would fit into their bills. Ostriches dwarfed them all, one cock weighing a full three hundred pounds. In the course of that single day, eight different secretary birds would stomp and stalk the grass looking for puff adders, mambas, and cobras, and even less dangerous snakes than that. Each would eventually succeed and fly off to a low tree limb, trailing a dead snake from its beak. With plovers by the hundreds and passerine birds by the scores of thousands, the total number of individuals would be almost astronomical by midafternoon. In all, well over two million vertebrate animals would appear that day on the one plateau in a stunning variety of sizes, shapes, and colors.

The vast quantities of dung the mammals and birds produced supported hundreds of millions of insects, and to prey upon them there was an astounding population of spiders, between two and three million of them to each acre of savannah. Some stalked and pounced, others spun their webs, although they were nearly blind in all eight of their eyes to anything but light and shadow. They would create miracles of intricate architecture stretched between blades of grass. Their silk manufactured for that purpose would exceed the tensile strength of steel wire.

The elephants soon began to spread out, pulling clumps of grass free of the earth, swinging them back and forth, whacking them against their forelegs to rid the roots of as much tooth-destroying grit as possible. But there were unexpected participants in the scene. Off among the trees, two men dressed in rags—their feet bound in strips of cloth and leather—crouched low, and studied the plain, watching the elephants move out into the open and begin to feed. Silently, signaling to each other, the men mentally weighed each tusk they saw and considered its probable worth. They were unarmed, but they knew where armed men waited in a cave and cooked chunks of fresh impala meat in an old coffee can over a small fire of twigs and moss. The scouts would be paid only pennies for their information, but they were part of a bush culture where even pennies could buy wonderful things that came from the cities. Such things could buy a wife or settle a nagging debt and could make a man important among his own people. Commerce involving money was not really a part of their culture yet, but it was coming. They were touched by it, for they wanted many things their fellow tribesmen did not have. Before commerce can flourish, before simple people open *dukas*—small sheds that serve as

78

Puff adders are among the most dangerous snakes, but secretary birds prey on them and other snakes without harm to themselves. ❖

shops in Africa—and buy and sell, there must be greed, and this the men had already learned.

The ivory that grew from the elephants' faces opened avenues for the scouts. In their eyes the beasts did not exist as living things about which one could have feelings.

The men with the guns, sophisticated automatic weapons manufactured for the old Soviet Union, would move out after they had eaten their impala meat and smoked from their small store of tobacco in pipes that they carved themselves and often discarded. These men traveled light. That slight delay would give the elephants enough time to settle down. Despite their intelligence, elephants can be lulled by a peaceful period into an easy state of mind. Warm sun, good grass, a plentiful supply of water, a wind without the smell of enemies upon it can make them vulnerable. The men who hunt them know how to approach so that their scent isn't carried to the herd on the wind.

The scouts told the poachers about one large bull that had come up to the cows as the animals came out of the forest. He carried very large tusks and was of great value, worth another coin or two at least.

The guns the men would use have a strange and complex history. In World War II a peasant boy from Siberia was wounded in a tank battle. While he was convalescing, he made drawings for a light, extremely reliable automatic weapon that was simple to manufacture yet could make a single infantryman as deadly as an assault team. The plans for the gun slowly worked their way up through the Soviet bureaucracy, and in time a prototype of the AK 47, or Kalashnikov gun, emerged and fulfilled its promise. Millions of the guns have now been manufactured, and they come from factories in China, Russia, and what was formerly Czechoslovakia. The AK 47 is the weapon of choice for terrorists and poachers and their political kin.

Hundreds of thousands of these guns are found under thatch mats in grass and dung huts, and buried, wrapped in raw animal hides, in shallow graves near villages. Although there are newer versions in Europe that can fire smaller, faster, even more deadly projectiles, the ones in the hands of elephant poachers are bad enough. They are in fact devastating.

The AK 47 weighs less than nine and a half pounds. Its magazine holds thirty rounds that launch a full-jacketed projectile 7.62 millimeters in diameter at a velocity of two thousand three hundred fifty feet per second. The gun can fire at a rate of six hundred rounds a minute, and the effect, even when the gun is held by mediocre marksmen, is to spray death like water from a hose. Four men so armed can approach an elephant herd and at almost nine hundred yards tear the animals apart, unzip them as they rake them with automatic fire.

The Siberian youth who had nearly died at the hands of the German invaders created his gun to protect his own country. But now the gun is being used to destroy the great animals of the world.

An AK 47 costs almost two thousand dollars to buy from regular arms' dealers, but in an effort to disrupt the politics of Africa, they have been made available and are traded for as little as a pack of cigarettes each.

The men who kill elephants to hack tusks from their

faces with *pangas*, or machetes, or even chain saws no longer make use of the ivory themselves. Their ancestors did, but the white gold is now too valuable for that. Highly placed military and political figures in capital cities, who speak to the press by day and decry the decimation of African wildlife and praise tourism, send their trucks at night to collect the ivory from secret places where the poachers wait. So valuable is the ivory that even helicopters may be used when the area where it has been hoarded is remote enough. The poachers, like the scouts who report to them, are paid pennies for their labor. The generals, colonels, and politicians collect the real money when the ivory is finally sold by the ton at auction and then shipped to Tokyo and Hong Kong for warehousing.

The elephants that moved in peace out onto the plateau were pawns in a complex game of history, greed, and commerce.

❖ ❖ ❖

But there were other scouts in the forest below the plateau that day. From high in a tree they had climbed thirty hours before, two of them watched the elephant spotters return. When they were certain they would not be seen, they slithered down the tree on the far side facing away from the cave's entrance. They slipped back through the bush, and silent as snakes, moved a third of a mile to where an antipoaching patrol of twelve men lay dug in, hidden and waiting. The news that the elephant spotters had returned was passed from man to man, and the patrol set aside its camouflage of brush and netting and began inching forward.

The patrol arrived behind some bushes just as the poachers and their spotters came out of the cave, blinked at the brightness of the sun, and started off toward the plateau. The patrol spread out so that each man would arrive at the edge of the vast clear area from a different place.

The shoot-on-sight order had been issued to the patrol two years before and had not been seriously resisted by the highly placed men for whom the poachers worked. They didn't worry about the fate of their employees, and speaking out against the order would have made them conspicuous.

The antipoaching patrol's order to kill on sight was essential to the men's own survival. They carried retired British .303 Enfield rifles, most of which had been released by the military at the end of World War I. The Enfield is accurate enough, quite accurate in fact, but unless used in an ambush, it is antiquated in a world of automatic weapons. When many more antipoaching men were being killed than poachers were, the game plan was changed. With slow but accurate fire from several different angles, the patrol would eliminate the poachers who could only ineffectively spray a forest that surrounded them once they reached the clear area of the plateau. The AK 47's advantage as a weapon requires it to have a target, and there are none when you are standing out in the open, ringed by trees and bushes.

When the two scouts and the four poachers emerged from the brush, the wind was exactly right, for it came from the elephants to them. They began to stalk, moving closer to ensure killing all the animals with tusks.

The lead man knelt and raised his gun, and then a bird call was heard. It was a junglelike sound, a signal, and in the moment it took for the poachers to realize what was happening, three of them died, their scouts with them. The one remaining poacher was far too seriously wounded to crawl away. A dozen old Enfields barked and barked again. Just before dying, one poacher, with his finger on the trigger of his AK 47, emptied its thirty rounds into the sky and then into the ground, as he rolled over and saw the world fill with shadows and then become black with his own death.

The explosive gunfire was a shattering disturbance on the plateau, and thousands of animals took flight. Those that could went into the sky and spiraled away with frantic wing beats, while those without wings fled across the broken ground. The elephants spun around, seeking the source of the sudden, crashing volley, and then, shrilling loudly, moved off with the rest. They stopped a mile and a half away and shuffled in circles, their ears, tails, and trunks extended. Then the lead cow entered the trees, moved down a trail that was worn deep into the ground by millennia of use, and soon the herd was gone.

The plateau was silent as the patrol members moved out of the bushes onto the grass. They turned the poachers over, took their guns and ammunition, and left them for the scavengers to clear away. The one badly injured man looked up with pleading eyes. He did not want to wait for the hyenas to come cackling after treasure. The patrol had other places to go and more similar work to do. It could not carry a dying man even if he had been one of their own. Life in the bush makes its own special demands. Men who go to the bush and match their own wits against creatures truly born of it must make adjustments in their values that would not be understood in more refined places, and openly condemned.

One of the men in the patrol looked at the surviving poacher with some small measure of pity. It was a brief moment, a passing exchange only, and then a single additional shot echoed through the nearby forest. The elephants heard it as they moved down the hill on the far side, away from the sour flamingo lake, and for a moment or two they walked just a little faster. They were openly upset and would be for hours to come.

The explosion had startled Ndovu as much as it had the other members of his herd. If he had been physically capable of jumping, he would have. Inside, in fact, his heart rate did jump, and a surge of stimulating chemicals had been released into his bloodstream. The reserve he might need at any moment for great exertions was ready.

Before he moved away in terror, Ndovu registered three smells he would never be able to forget. There was the odor of the elephants themselves, which changed in the excitement and fear. There was the stink of burning gunpowder mixed with gun oil, and then there was the pungent smell of unwashed men. Ndovu had been well warned. He had felt the terror sweep through the herd like a bolt of electricity. He had not only been startled himself, felt the pain of loud noises, but smelled the stink of fear. His lesson was an expensive one, but the true cost of it on this occasion had been borne by animals of another species. This time he and his herd had survived and were well away.

8

FIRST CHALLENGES

Several years had passed since the poachers had shattered the solitude of the high African plateau. Ndovu shuffled forward through the ground mist as it tumbled around his feet and rose to the level of his belly. He shook his head,  and his ears flopped against his shoulders with loud slapping sounds. The currents of air that his ears created eddied the mist in front of him, and he pushed on through their circular patterns. The yellow dawn bathed the area and made him glow like a dull golden apparition in a world of transient blue and gray. He made deep sounds in his throat and soft shrilling sounds through his trunk. He swung his trunk up and ahead and periodically sampled the air. He was at ease but alert as he waited for the sun to warm the world.

It was not a good time for the young bull. He was now nine years old and already starting on his third set of molars that had inched forward from the back of his jaws. He weighed two and a half tons and had reached puberty. Although there would be no chance of his mating for several years at least, he was producing sperm and with that there had been marked changes in his behavior.

About the time Ndovu had been born, a very much older cow in the herd who was only very distantly related to his mother had also given birth to a calf, an undersized female. Actually, the old cow was just about at the very end of her calf-bearing years, close to fifty years old. Most cows are not fertile that long.

The old cow had not been well either during the nearly twenty-two months she had carried her slowly developing calf, nor during the months of her calf's infancy. The cow's coronary arteries, the vessels that carried oxygenated blood back to the heart muscles themselves, had begun building up plates and disks of calcium salt. The vessels slowly lost their flexibility and as they became rigid they became increasingly fragile, all of this as her infant's term drew to a close. She was sick immediately after having given birth and the normally elastic fibers in her artery walls continued to degenerate. It was not a condition that would ever reverse itself. The old cow was prematurely and permanently ill. She had not suffered excessive trauma, had not been invaded by dangerous parasites or organisms. Her mother and grandmother had both died as young animals, neither having reached fifty. Her genes carried the terms of her mortality. Each genetic package, whether in elephant or human being, carries along with everything else a death sentence. Unless events preempt it, it is inexorable.

Somehow the old cow managed to hang on for four years after she had her calf, although she tired easily and often lagged behind the rest of the herd. There were times when she was as much as a full day's march behind the others, and often another cow or two would linger as well, staying with her to help her guide and protect her infant. Fortunately, she was able to produce sufficient milk for her daughter through the period that the baby depended on it. Then one day shortly after her daughter was four, the walls of her major vessel ruptured. There was no warning. First a tiny crack appeared, and that quickly became a gaping hole forced open by the pressure of the blood coming through the artery. Her heart weighed almost thirty pounds and pumped blood through the vessel with enormous pressure. The aneurysm allowed blood to gush out into her chest cavity, and her heart faltered briefly and then simply stopped. She appeared stunned for a moment, then seemed to try to lie down. Before she could, however, she fell and she was dead.

The rest of the herd had been moving ahead but sensed the unusual behavior of the old cow. A quiet and gentle animal, she had been very popular with the other cows, and they came back to her. They grumbled and moaned and a few blasted shrilly, encouraging her to stand. They closed in and rubbed their trunks over her body. Several used their tusks to try to get her up. The old cow's female calf rubbed against her mother and then rested her trunk on the great left foreleg. The smaller animal looked confused, trying to understand her mother's strange behavior. Nothing she had learned so far could help her.

A half a dozen times other cows tried to get the old cow to stand and move off with them. When they failed, they forced the calf away from her station, but she always circled back to maintain physical contact with her mother. The old cow had been the absolute center of her world. There was no way she could understand that that had now changed forever.

As if expecting the popular old cow to change her mind about dying, most of the herd stayed near her body through the remainder of that day, throughout the long night, and well into the afternoon of the next day. Half the herd moved ahead and began feeding about a mile away. The other half, though, including Ndovu and his mother, stayed with the body. It was a hot day, and by late that second afternoon the elephants' sensitive sense of smell convinced them that their companion of so many years would never rise again and that waiting had become futile. The calf stood with her trunk draped across her mother's tusk, and only when she was clearly about to be left alone did she amble after the other cows.

The signs of death in Africa are always unmistakable. There is a kind of network on land and in the sky. The event of death, particularly in a larger animal, is never a secret for long. Over forty hyenas had gathered at a safe distance before the night ended, and they were becoming noisier and bolder every minute. They had tired of their quiet, seemingly patient deathwatch and now they wanted to feed. Time and again they had been scattered, sent away cackling and yelping by one or two patrolling cows. Nearly seventy vultures had gathered overhead and circled and dipped on the thermal currents that the warming surface of the earth provided. Almost half of them had received the news before sunset of the day the cow died, and they had waited through the night in trees no more than a hundred feet away. They knew the dead animal was theirs. They only had to wait out the protective cows, whose resolve would fade before their own. Now they were airborne and watched the scene below with ever-increasing interest. Every time they landed and tried to approach the carcass, the other cows sent them flapping away, hissing with ungainly rage and fear.

But as the last cow turned away to move off with her herd mates, the first vultures were already standing on the dead cow's shoulder. Jackals of two species, black-backed and side-striped, waited too. They knew their time would come as well.

Ndovu's mother approached the rest of the herd with two calves instead of one. She no longer had to provide milk for either, but she could offer comfort and counsel. She would teach two calves how to be elephants, not just one. The female calf had simply come to her side as they moved away toward the main body of the herd, and the matter was settled. The adoption had been that easy.

For some months after the orphaned calf had rejoined the herd and Ndovu had been called upon to share his mother, it had seemed to rankle. He was quite capable of jealousy, but when any signs of sibling rivalry were seen, Ndovu's mother was quick to interfere. Rivalry within the herd at any level is always discouraged. Har-

If an elephant calf is orphaned, other cows in the herd will take over the protection of the young animal. ❖

mony above all is required of any animals who want to stay with the herd.

So for almost five years Ndovu shared his mother, although at times without much grace. He kept himself within bounds, however, because instinctively he feared arousing her anger. Rejection by an elephant mother is a trauma all elephants try to avoid. The cow calf was docile and obedient, and after a few days of initial confusion responded to Ndovu's mother as readily as she had to her own. In time she and Ndovu developed an easier relationship. It wasn't long before it seemed to Ndovu and to his mother as if the little cow had always been there. If Ndovu had been capable of thinking about the situation and could have exercised options, he would surely have remained an only calf during his pre-puberty years. That was beyond him, however, so he made the best of the altered situation until it no longer mattered.

There was another factor that Ndovu had to contend with. At every stage, elephants must make social adjustments, for nothing stays the same always. Even the herd itself is dynamic and changing. New calves are born, natural and unnatural deaths occur, and calves grow while adults age and die or simply vanish. Within Ndovu's herd was a bull only days younger than himself who was destined to be as mammoth as Ndovu was becoming. They were both animals of enormous energy and spirit. Both were distinctly dominant types and eyed each other suspiciously even while they were still with their mothers.

Both young bulls engaged in the testing, pushing contests with the other calves who were growing up around them, but somehow, when these two young bulls entwined trunks, it was different. Their eyes grew a little harder and their throat sounds were more intense. They both seemed to understand that a real contest existed that would one day have to try them both.

By the time they were eight, Ndovu and Challenger eyed each other with mounting suspicion and came together several times a day to shove and goad and face off. Their respective mothers knew what was coming. They had seen it happen before. The signs were unmistakable. Ndovu and Challenger would have to be pushed out of the herd sooner than usual, because although they were still just in the nuisance stage as they passed their eighth birthdays, they would soon become a threat to the young calves that had been born after them. Alone, either one would have been fine for at least another two or three years. The alert and dominating cows could have controlled them, but the two together were edging out of control and couldn't be tolerated for much longer. It was an impossible situation and threatened the peace of the group, something the cows would not allow to get very far.

One day there was a real clash. Somehow the almost hourly game they had been playing had gotten out of hand, and shrilling loudly, the two young bulls stepped back and charged into each other with full force. Ndovu went to his knees from the impact. When they withdrew and charged again, it was Challenger who went down. The cows with calves moved away first, some hurrying to get their infants to safety. The cows without calves formed a circular barrier around the two young bulls until the most vulnerable herd members had been led well away. Then they too quietly withdrew, leaving the two young gladiators to themselves.

The two bulls pushed, shoved, goaded each other with their tusks that now were about eight inches in length, and jockeyed for position. They apparently didn't notice that they were alone in a dusty basin of an ancient lake bed. The herd had withdrawn to a papyrus marsh about two miles away. The bulls stirred up clouds of acrid dust as they continued to jostle and jockey and seek advantage. They were evenly matched, however, and only succeeded in exhausting each other.

The contest had, at its core, disputes still to come in the years ahead. Access to accepting females, breeding priority was what it was all about; among elephants such matters are sorted out well in advance. However, the young bulls would resolve their differences in another way. They would eventually move apart and seek other herds with other cows. That would be good, for they were related distantly and carried many of the same genes. They shared not one but two great-grandparents, and it would be better that they brought the genes for size and aggressiveness to different breeding lines as far apart as possible.

Ndovu and Challenger represented a major problem that has come to exist for elephants. Their species has been so heavily poached, with the emphasis on huge males with large tusks, and so much of their habitat has been preempted, that dominant males tend to have far too many breeding opportunities in limited areas for the good of the species as a whole. In this case, nature would resolve the quandary by forcing these two gene carriers, distant cousins, apart. There was no real animosity between the two, just the need within each to dominate and to be distrustful of any other bull displaying the same need.

When the two bulls had exhausted themselves and each other (for it really had been a test of endurance more than anything else), they began looking for their herd. It was several miles away, but they had no difficulty in finding it. They approached, Challenger in the lead, Ndovu only a few steps behind, to find not the usual welcoming sounds and touches, but a wall of cold rejection and indifference.

As Ndovu approached his mother, she swung sharply to face him. She flapped her ears in a very intimidating way and shook her head from side to side. She blasted air through her trunk swirling the dust at her feet. Ndovu didn't try to move up to her, but took her cue and stayed back. He knew the signs. When the herd moved off, the two young bulls trailed behind. Challenger had received a cool reception from his mother as well. Somehow the two bulls were aware but didn't understand. Something was happening to them, but they didn't have the intellectual capacity to determine what it was. Ndovu and Challenger were being squeezed out.

Five days after the first of their contests that exceeded herd tolerance, it happened again. This time when they had exhausted themselves, the herd was difficult to find. It was almost seven miles away. A week later it was nine miles away and the reception they received bordered on being openly hostile.

Ten days later their tempers flared yet again and when the contest wound down, the herd was gone and they didn't try to find it. The two young bulls were large enough to care for themselves. They knew what to eat and how to find water, and they were too big for even the lion, the largest of the local predators, to test. They turned into the mist and keeping a hundred feet or so apart, on parallel tracks, moved down toward a river that flowed less than a mile away. They could smell it and now knew enough to follow their own senses rather than to depend on a cow to lead them.

Over the ensuing weeks and months, they traveled together, yet still remained apart. They had given up the comfort of elephant touch temporarily, but they no longer engaged in their usual shoving and jabbing contests. That was because there were no females around to arouse the testing of each other. They had quickly changed from highly dependent, extremely social, even gregarious animals into grumpy, solitary young bulls who stayed near each other out of habit, but were not really together either.

One day when they were bathing in a river about a thousand yards apart, Ndovu stepped up the bank across the river from where they had come and walked toward a line of purple hills barely visible on the horizon. Challenger heard his opponent, caught a message on the wind that he was now alone, and went back to spraying water over his back. He would eventually go back up the bank by which they had approached the river and wander in familiar territory. The two bulls would never see each other again. Their need for dominance had driven them apart just as it had triggered the cows to send them away from their herd. Eventually Challenger would rejoin the herd into which he had been born for brief conjugal visits, but Ndovu would seek another one far away. Now his time to wander had begun.

9

THE ASKARI
AND
THE RAID

Ndovu moved down the easy side of the cut and stopped to feed briefly on some tender new branch growth just before the tall, tufted needlegrass began. Then he moved on out into the grass and began feeding in earnest.  He was busy at his harvesting chore for nearly an hour before a wind shift told him he was not alone. He could not see the intruder upon his solitude, but he was still able to locate and identify him. He was a lone elephant, and although the wind direction had kept his secret, he had been sensing Ndovu since he first emerged from the opening in the hill.

Ndovu, the more aggressive and assertive of the two, flipped his trunk and followed the scent trail upwind until he was only a few yards from the other bull. This was an animal wholly unknown to him, but there was no challenge and the two young bulls came together.

They brushed against each other, checked out the areas under each other's tail and between their hind legs with inquiring trunks to be certain of sex and to store a scent memory for possible later identification. Then they stood together in the sun. They were, it seemed, happy to have found each other, or at least they experienced positive reactions to not being alone.

The bull Ndovu encountered was two years older than he was, but smaller and less aggressive. Although mild in manner, he had come to a time when his herd could no longer hold him, and he had wandered off. There had been a bull like Ndovu in the herd who was constantly testing Wanderer, bullying him because of the cows, and Wanderer had taken the course of least resistance. He was lonely though, and eager for some of the socializing on which he had been raised. Ndovu too was lonely, but had seemingly become resigned to his fate.

By late that afternoon Ndovu and Wanderer were familiar with each other and reconditioned to companionship. They didn't interact much; it was simply a matter of being together. Ndovu, because he was larger and more aggressive, was easily the leader of the pair. Without resistance Wanderer followed where Ndovu led, although that meant giving up the options he had been exercising since he first went off on his own. There were no commands, no insistence. Ndovu just did what he had been doing since he had been ostracized. In a way the two young bulls switched roles. Although Ndovu was twenty-six months younger than Wanderer, it was Wanderer who became the askari, the companion guard to his junior. It is normally a role played by younger bulls to older more experienced animals.

Elephants prefer to live with others of their species, whether it is two or fifty or more. ❖

Ndovu moved along apparently aimlessly, and fed, and Wanderer stayed close. There was water nearby and they went to that, drank, bathed, and then moved to where the needlegrass gave over to an area of hairy bluestem grass and a dozen other species as well. They came to a grove of acacias and leveled two trees between them. It was an easy relationship based on mutual needs. Neither animal had liked being alone. Solitude had confused them and made them uneasy.

As they wandered on their third day together, they began to encounter strange smells, at least one of which was disturbing to Ndovu. It was the smell of man. The only other time that he had encountered it had been explosively traumatic, up on the plateau beyond the soda lake of the flamingos. Still, the man-smell was faint and there were other odors too, which were distinctively enticing. The two elephants were in fact approaching a village just at dusk, and they circled the area, turned back, and circled it again. It lay beyond a heavy stand of trees, but the two elephants could locate it by smell and sound. Since neither had encountered a human settlement before, they had no guide, nothing to tell them what to do.

The odors that attracted them were crops. The villagers with their small plots were cultivating maize and millet and sugarcane, and they had tree crops too: oranges and bananas and one lone mango tree. Ndovu and Wanderer did not know these scents, but they were sweet and attractive and drew them on.

After dark the two young bulls approached the cultivated areas through the large grove of trees. They could not know that an electric fence had been strung around the gardens, and that a small diesel-powered generator fed its invisible strands with enough power to surprise an elephant unpleasantly. Ndovu touched it first and then Wanderer. In succession they gave shrill snorts, the equivalent in elephants of yelps of surprise. They backed off quickly, Ndovu shaking his head violently. It had been more startling than actually painful, but it had been decidedly unpleasant. The farmers in their huts grunted with satisfaction when they heard what sounded like elephants in terror, and listened to the two young bulls crash off through the trees beyond their gardens. They had several lines of defense, which was a necessary precaution if they were to raise crops at all. From long and bitter personal and tribal experience they knew that even a few elephants—even one, in fact— could destroy a whole year's crop in a few hours. The electric fence was just their first line, and often with some elephants it was enough. With some elephants, but not all.

Ndovu and Wanderer moved back through the trees and out across the savannah. They were gone before the first light that brought the farmers out of their huts to examine their plots and estimate what if any damage had been done. They smiled and called to each other with satisfaction when they determined that their first line had held. They wondered, though, if the two apparently young elephants would be back. They could determine that the elephants were young not by the size of their footprints but by the footprints' lack of wear and the age lines. Even Wanderer was already as large as some adult elephants ever got, and Ndovu was considerably larger, but their tracks were youthful, their feet not heavily worn from decades of use. The farmers could tell that, and they wondered too if they would have to break the law and shoot these potential marauders as they had others from time to time.

Early the next evening Ndovu and Wanderer were back in the forested area just beyond the cultivated plots. At the equator, dawn and dusk are not drawn-out events. It is suddenly light, and just as suddenly, at the end of the day, it is dark. Shortly after the light had gone from the wooden area, the two potential raiders were moving toward the village. With uncanny precision they positioned themselves at the fence line where the wire had stung them the night before. Ndovu feared the wire, but was drawn by the new odors beyond. It was a case of negative and positive incentives. Whichever proved stronger would determine the pair's actions in the minutes immediately ahead.

Ndovu probed with his tusks, and although the smell of man was stronger than it had been the previous evening, he accepted that too, although it would be the last time he would ever do so. Somehow, by experimenting, Ndovu discovered that his tusks did not conduct electricity. He touched the dreaded wire and nothing happened. He was in the process of stripping the wire from the post when the explosions occurred. For the second time in his life gunfire erupted nearby, this time at virtually point-blank range. Wanderer fell against Ndovu, killed instantly by the three bullets that crashed into his skull. Ndovu was untouched, although he was in a state of shock. The angle from which the ambush exploded

Elephants easily uproot whole trees in their quest for the vast amount of food they require each day. ❖

kept Ndovu hidden behind his companion and so one elephant lived and another died there by the fence at the edge of the cultivated plot. It had been a matter of luck and nothing more. Ndovu went quickly back into the forest, and then he was gone.

10

NEW
IMPERATIVES

Alone again, as he would be for the next seven months, Ndovu wandered. He was more alert than ever, careful, suspicious, quick to anger, and therefore potentially dangerous. His recent experience outside the farming village  had put his entire nervous system on full alert. New situations, he now knew, are always to be approached with extreme caution. He would never forget that, just as he would never forget the smell of human beings and those other dreadful scents he had experienced for the first time high up on the plateau. He would always be afraid of the two distinctive smells of gun oil and burning powder, and would be angered by them.

Wanderer had died at his side in that terrifying instant when gunfire had exploded among the trees in the night near the village. Ndovu's strength, size, and stamina would stand for something in times of danger and stress, but it would be better for him not to test himself more often than was necessary. The handsome young bull who had been full of the elephant's equivalent of hubris, of self-pride, had fallen off the ledge to his death above the soda lake in a moment of carelessness. In fact he had been far more daring than Ndovu had been at that age, and had he lived, he would have been even larger and perhaps even tougher.

Ndovu was as capable of misjudgment as that young bull had been. Animals that survive carelessness are protected by a distant star, perhaps, but not by their wits, at least not when they are young. Failure in judgment is always a possible cause of mortality, and although it is more so when animals are young, it is always a potential threat. Ndovu would have to skirt an endless parade of opportunities that would conspire to cause him to fail himself and his species.

A week after Wanderer's death Ndovu came to a broad grassy expanse after spending a particularly dark night back among some yellow fever trees. He quickly caught the scent of what was clearly another elephant. With his trunk and ears out he moved in a wide circle, huffing, squealing his alert sound, and seeking further clues. About a half mile away another lone bull caught the briefest of clues to Ndovu's presence when the surface wind shifted through the grass. Stranger too moved in a circle trying to catch further information about this new event in his life. He was just a year older than Ndovu and was also an outcast because he had offended two old cows in his herd and had been crowded out by their intolerance.

Ndovu and Stranger managed to collect enough data about each other over a period of several hours to know that neither was a threat to the other. They periodically fed, circled on air sampling missions, and then fed again, but never came much closer to each other. Neither bull could see the other, but each was aware of the presence of a stranger. Although members of a highly gregarious species, this was not a very social period in either of their lives. They fed between a half and three-quarters of a mile apart most of the night and continued their pattern of circling and feeding through the next day and then the next as well. They each made seven trips to a nearby river during that period, but they used different trails to get to the bank in places where it could be negotiated. They could hear each other splashing and blowing on the four occasions when they were in the river at the same time, but they still remained apart. They stopped and listened to each other and regularly tested the air, but had little more communion than that. On one occasion Ndovu blasted a high, shrill call, and Stranger quickly answered. They both grumbled to themselves after that, but there it ended.

On the fourth morning, Ndovu came out into a flat area where protein-rich beck grass grew, and began feeding. He was more relaxed about Stranger being in the area than he had been the three previous mornings, and he began grazing toward the clump of trees where Stranger had been spending his nights. But there were no fresh clues. Eventually Ndovu came upon one- and two-day-old droppings about the size of bowling balls. He tested the air above them with his trunk, pushed them around with his forefoot, and tested their scent

Elephants communicate with one another with moans, grumbles, shrill blasts, and trumpeting warning roars. ❖

again. The information they offered coincided with what he already knew about Stranger, but Stranger had moved off in the dark.

Ndovu stayed with the beck grass for two more days, moving into groves of trees for most of the dark hours, but visiting the river under both the sun and the moon. Then his body urged him to seek other kinds of food.

Ndovu's anatomy limited his feeding habits. His mouth when fully open was still amazingly small for an animal his size. It was virtually hidden by the base of his trunk. He could not extend his tongue beyond his lower lip, although it was large and mobile and muscular. The strength and mobility of his trunk compensated for all of that, however, and he depended on it for his survival.

In a grove a dozen miles away he found a variety of fruit-bearing trees. Near a river several döum palms grew with huge, spreading, far-reaching substems high above the ground. Their fruit was ripe, and Ndovu singled out a particularly tall tree and tested it with his trunk. The fruit was well beyond his reach, and he extended his trunk as far up the main stem as possible. He pushed so hard he was able to move his tongue over the bark, and then he encircled the stem with his trunk. He took a single step back and coiled his trunk tightly under his chin and leaned forward, bringing his forehead into contact with the tree. He leaned and withdrew again and again, setting up a swaying motion that was greater near the top of the tree where the fronds and the fruit were than it was below. Ndovu kept at it until fruit began raining down on him, scattering for yards around. When he was standing on a carpet of the three-

An elephant's trunk is a remarkably sensitive all-purpose tool that can be used to pick up anything from a peanut to a tree. ❖

cornered orange-brown fruit, he stopped and began his harvest. His trunk searched, encircling the fruit and carrying each piece to his mouth. He moved a few steps only when all of the fruit within his reach had been consumed. In a couple of hours he demolished the carpet and moved off.

Within an hour he was feeding again on a marula tree, the plant known to science as *Sclerocarya*. The fruit of the tree had ripened about a week and a half earlier and bushels had already fallen to the ground. Ndovu sought out the fallen fruits first, and when they were gone, he began swaying the tree itself, just as he had the mighty döum palm near the river course. Again fruit fell on him and around him, and again he fed, but this time there was a difference. The fruit of the marula quickly becomes overripe, and the ample liquid inside its tissues ferments. The more Ndovu fed, the drunker he became; and as he turned to move away, his front knees buckled and he went down on them. He was able to right himself, but he stumbled off, bumping into other trees as he tried to walk. A lilac-breasted roller rocketed past, and Ndovu somehow felt that was threatening to him. When the magnificently colored bird landed in a low tree nearby, Ndovu charged it in an ill-controlled rush. He pushed right over the tree, flattening it, tearing its roots from the ground. The roller was well away before Ndovu's badly orchestrated show of strength did little but kill a tree and some small arthropods that lived among its root hairs.

Stumbling on, Ndovu charged a group of six zebras passing en route to the river. They scattered briefly, disdainfully, and then came together again to resume their short trek. Ndovu charged some waterbucks, then a bachelor herd of impalas with as much reason and with as little success as he had the roller and the zebras. He was easy to avoid, and he finally gave it up and came to rest against a tall eucalyptus tree. A great eagle-owl blinked down with disapproval as Ndovu's weight made the tree tremble. Nearby, a pair of malachite kingfishers flitted from branch to branch watching the drunken giant blow dust clouds with short, sharp rushes of air from his trunk. An incredibly arrayed amethyst sunbird, velvety black with a metallic green cap and rosy purple throat markings, trembled in the air, and then shot by, passing within inches of Ndovu's face. He didn't see it. He was struggling to remain upright and conscious.

To suggest that Ndovu was trying to maintain his dignity would reach beyond the probable facts of elephant mentality, but to a stranger looking on, it could have seemed that way. Most of the animals around him had encountered drunken elephants before, and many knew that he was, for the moment, largely bluff and bluster and too poorly coordinated to be of real concern. Animals that share the elephants' range know how to avoid the giants when the marula fruit is ripe. It is generally the only time they need to concern themselves with elephant affairs. It is a time when good neighbors turn bad.

Ndovu was confused and dislocated in time, thoroughly intoxicated from gorging on the fermented marula fruit. Two dik-diks, antelope not very much larger than rabbits, kept back under some low brush and watched the spectacle of the tottering animal. Ndovu de-

Many animals, including elephants, will become drunk after eating overripe, fermenting fruit. When they do so, other animals try to avoid them. ❖

tected their presence and tried to pull himself away from the eucalyptus tree and charge these seemingly life-threatening forces as well. It was too much work to move, he was far too wobbly, and he decided against the adventure. He passed a mighty, rolling blast of intestinal gases instead. The eagle-owl continued to look at him in seeming disapproval and finally moved over to another tree nearby.

Ndovu remained virtually frozen in place for almost six hours, and then at dusk he moved down to the river. He was sick and still feeling terrible, but he would not pass up opportunities to gorge on fermented marula fruit in the future. Like all of his kind, he apparently enjoyed such interludes now and then. Few other species could risk being so out of control and confused even for moments, much less for several hours. Lions and leopards will not try to test even a drunken elephant, for there is always the danger that others will be nearby.

❖ ❖ ❖

Ndovu had reached his teenage years. Had he been a less aggressive animal, he probably would have remained with his mother and the other cows. A number of his contemporaries were still with the herd. Perhaps if Challenger hadn't been there to test Ndovu, he would not have been as aggressive and troublesome. Perhaps a herd periodically produces two challenging young bulls so that their genes will be pushed farther afield.

As he moved along the base of a well-forested hill, Ndovu heard sounds he had never encountered before. There were metallic clunking noises, strange animal sounds, and a shrill, rhythmic whistling that did not seem as if it had an animal origin at all. The new sounds merged, blended into a sound fabric that seemed natural to the land, even if it was new to the young bull.

Masai herdsmen were passing, moving several hundred goats, donkeys, and sheep toward a watering hole only a mile away, and they maintained a constant whistling song that kept their animals together. The tall, lean teenagers with their dung-matted hair carried long spears and hardwood, knobbed throwing sticks. Their clothing consisted of a single length of red fabric draped seemingly without purpose across one shoulder and rather casually gathered around their thighs. If threatened or challenged in any way, the youths would drop their cloths and run naked through the bush. Some wore a kind of leather or rubber sandal and others were barefoot. It hardly mattered, for these young men were as tough and resilient as the earth and the weather and the animals among whom they moved without fear. Lions knew their smell and avoided them. They could throw their knobbed sticks with enough force and accuracy to knock a bird out of the sky seventy feet overhead. They could drive their spears deep into a slender hardwood tree with an incredible running, overhand throw.

The Masai are flat-bellied men and women whose bodies seem to be constructed of stretched steel and leather thongs. The men are vain, chauvinistic, merciless toward outsiders who challenge them, and they know their way is the only way, and they do not covet what their lifestyle denies them. They live when they live and are dead when they die and are resigned to that design.

The Masai never were as warlike as legend would have them. They are essentially peaceful, nomadic pasturalists, but they are tough and just about fearless. They will kill anything, anyone, human or animal, if their flocks are threatened in any way. Their stock—donkeys, goats, and sheep, coupled with their vast cattle holdings—constitutes their wealth, bride purchase capabilities, as well as their identity. It is the pivot on which their culture turns. It is their breath, their blood, their power to reproduce themselves, their purpose for being. If you rob a Masai of his livestock, you rob him of himself and that he cannot tolerate. From the day he is circumcised in his early teens, a Masai is a *moran*, or warrior, and has a lifelong license to kill offenders of his people's wealth and being.

Ndovu was attracted by the strange herds of bleating and baaing animals. Concentrating on their strange smells and sounds, at first he didn't detect the man-smell. He had emerged from the lowest cluster of trees at the very bottom of the hill and had discovered the Masai youths just moments after they saw him. The steely young men were watching, signaling alert signs to one another, not certain what the large young bull was going to do. Normally they would not be concerned with elephants unless they were bringing their flocks to a water hole and found a herd of the giants already in possession of it. This lone bull was different, though, for young men knew well that the behavior of herd-oriented animals like the elephant and cape buffalo is always uncertain when they are not with their own kind.

The moment Ndovu detected the man-smell, his ears went out to full width and he whirled left and then right. The youths knew the signs instantly. He was a dangerous animal. Ndovu blasted his powerful threat sound, his alarm note, and the parade of livestock passing in front of him bowed out away from him but kept flowing. The Masai morani began positioning themselves to throw their spears from several different directions simultaneously before sprinting into the trees and seeking cover. They knew the challenge had been made and, in their own way, they welcomed it. Young morani are always seeking means to assert their manhood. Maidens await young men who throw their spears well and who do not shrink from danger. It is a selection system and keeps the hard Masai as tough as they must be.

When he sensed that he was being surrounded, Ndovu charged. Two unfortunate goats immediately in front of him were trampled and died instantly, while several others were bumped and injured. It was mayhem. A single sheep stood staring in confusion as Ndovu picked her up in his trunk and threw her against a tree. Her back was broken. She and the lamb inside of her died soon, but not without pain.

Then the spears came. Strong, naked young men were trying to kill Ndovu. One spear lodged near the base of his trunk and caused him enormous pain. He roared, but was immediately distracted by a second spear that pinned his right ear to his neck. A third lodged briefly in his left shoulder, but encountered dense bone and soon fell to the ground as Ndovu whirled. His foot snapped its wooded shaft. A throwing stick, used for distraction, thudded below his left eye and another over his right. They hurt him, but did no real harm. They did serve their purpose, however. By the time he could focus his attention again on anything but the rain of offending objects, the men were gone. One was hundreds of yards to the right, on the original line of march, darting and whistling, gathering the scattered animals back into order. Some goats had already pushed on ahead and were at the water drinking. The three other young morani moved along behind the treeline, slightly up the slope of the hill, peering down frequently as they moved to see what the young bull would do next.

Ndovu stood dazed for a minute or two, then moved back into the trees well behind the points where the herdsmen had taken cover. Before he had gone a hundred feet, the two spears still in him were dislodged, and although he bled copiously, he suffered no mortal wounds. Ndovu had chosen an ill-advised course of action and had courted not instant death—he was too large for that and the arm of man too weak—but he had invited injuries that could have permanently disabled his trunk and led to a slow and painful death or crippled him in some other way. The herdsmen would not have attacked Ndovu if he had not attacked them or their flock. He had had options and he had chosen badly. Once again he had been close to death and had survived. Luck, not wit or skill, had spared him.

Ndovu moved through the trees away from the young morani and their flocks. Within an hour they would recover three of their four spears and all of their throwing sticks and would be attending their animals at the water hole. Later that evening, just before the end of the brief equatorial sunset, one of the Masai youths would drive his spear deep into the side of a hyena that would try to take a kid from the outskirts of their flock. The hyena would die slowly. The teenage guardian of his clan's wealth would watch in interest but without pity before recovering his bloodied spear for a second time in a single day. Two days later when the youths rejoined their people, the hyena would deserve only passing mention, but the news that a crazed elephant that killed goats and sheep was in the valley would cause a great deal of discussion. Word would spread, and people who had long treks to make would be alerted.

Fifteen miles from where Ndovu's third encounter with the man-smell had occurred, the young bull came upon a broad expanse of marshland and walked into the water until it nearly covered him. He would spend several weeks in the area without ever realizing the instinctive pattern of his behavior. Growing among the weeds was a form of fungus belonging to the group *Trichocomaceae*. Billions of the little plants reproduced and flourished there. One bore the familiar name *Penicillium*. Ndovu would bathe in the water and never move far from it until his wounds were healed. Elephants, it seems, discovered the antibiotic value of certain fungi before Alexander Fleming did.

Two and a half weeks into his healing time in the marsh, Ndovu detected a small herd of elephants that came regularly to the open water areas to bathe and to drink. There were two family groups, cows with three calves each of different ages, two unmated cows, and one partially grown bull who had somehow lost his mother and was still very submissive. Ndovu, still suspicious, stayed back where the plant growth was thickest, and listened and smelled them. They knew he was there too, but except for some light curiosity on the part of the young bull and one of the unmated cows, they paid little attention to the lone animal who shared their swamp.

The young cow, who was vaguely interested in the fact that Ndovu was near, was just coming into estrus, or heat. On occasion she urinated while on dry ground, leaving a large puddle before moving off. Ndovu came up out of the water, and with his trunk, minutely examined that puddle for several minutes. He stood over it, came back to it several times, and felt stirrings inside himself announcing a new compelling sensation. He didn't understand it, of course, but something was drawing him back toward others of his own kind. He wasn't quite ready to mate yet, but the time was approaching when using his maleness appropriately would be more important than displaying it. The small herd left the area of the marsh a few days before Ndovu did, and now he followed them, encountering the unmistakable urine puddles of the young cow several more times in the first week.

11

THE IMPERIAL GUARD

The broad savannah and the low hills through which Ndovu and the small herd with the enticing young cow moved was lush and fulfilling of all the elephants' needs. There were small rivers detectable to the elephants by smell and to  better-sighted animals by the serrated lines of trees which traced the me- andering water- courses along each bank. The seemingly end- less shades of green intensified in areas where water reached the surface, either in depressions or in channels that flowed with the land.

Clusters of trees stood back away from the rivers, and small lakes and ponds flowed off into broad expanses of marshland. Some bodies of water were surrounded by marsh, enclosed by growth so lush that the life-forms present defied counting. From the microscopic motes in both water and soil to large stands of papyrus with their great balled heads, to trees of many kinds, it was a huge area inhabited by many thousands of species of insects and arthropods, and hundreds of species of birds, some seasonal, some year-round residents. A single tree was a jungle, the root system of even a small plant a host to myriad forms of life.

East African crowned cranes, always at least in pairs but sometimes in aggregations of hundreds, moved around one pond. A few miles away hundreds of stately, black-and-white European storks, from as far away as Sweden and Siberia, ended their migration and winged in in aerial phalanxes to wait out the winter that engulfed their breeding range far from the African savannah.

Vultures of five or six species inhabited the area, worked it, used it, did their chores. There were the Ruppell's vultures that nested in cliffs no more than a score of miles to the east, and also white-backed, Nubian, white-headed, hooded, and Egyptian vultures. They constituted the basic vulture population, although on rare occasions when the wind was exactly right, the enormous lammergeyer, or bearded vulture, almost three and a half feet long and looking like a survivor of the prehistoric past, soared in from a stretch of cliffs nearly fifty miles away. The lammergeyer's roosting and nesting site in the cliffs could be seen for miles. Hundred-foot-long streaks of white and yellow excrement stained the cliffs. At the top of each of the enormous streaks, many of them centuries old, was inevitably a place where lammergeyers sat. Whole worlds of bacteria and minute arthropods lived in those streaks, depending on them to be constantly replenished. Each such brushstroke on the bare rock was a universe in itself.

With the help of a large population of marabou storks, animals extraordinary only in flight, the vultures redistributed the chemicals of life as predators and other natural forces made them available. Undigested and viable seeds were dropped by elephants. It is believed that the acid bath to which they have been subjected while passing through the elephant's digestive system chemically "cracks" them and makes them more likely to germinate. Vast numbers of dung beetles created small balls from the droppings and pushed them with their hind legs, walking backward at a precipitous angle. The beetles rolled their small hordes in all directions to depressions in the earth where they would lay their eggs and incidentally plant the seeds that had come with the elephants from ten miles away. Birds too carried seeds, spreading them over vast distances, leaving them in their droppings along the watercourses where the earth was soft and receptive. Other seeds were carried by the wind, and still others were carried along by the streams that meandered through the savannah. Often the seeds, as motes of flotsam, washed ashore on muddy banks and found rich beds waiting to engulf and nurture them. All of the earth was well dunged and intensely rich. The whole area was a vast, limitless garden that was constantly being renewed, fertilized, replanted, and readied for harvest. The scale was so vast that the seedbeds ran to the horizon and far beyond, because the land was not truly flat. The energy sent down by the sun and weather systems that sent the winds and the rains from thousands of miles away orchestrated it all. It was a vast basin, a dent in the earth awash in life.

Ndovu was a part of the system no less and no more than the spider that stalked the insect or the cheetah that ran down the gazelle. Ndovu would kill many millions of individual plants in his long lifetime of feeding, but he would distribute the seeds and the nutrients for many, many millions more.

In an area so rich in food and water, the number of mammals that gathered there was enormous. Giraffes, the tallest of all existing animals, generally stayed in areas where there were trees. Gerenuks, extremely delicate and graceful gazelles of many shades of cream and tan, and with long necks, fed in the same forests, while below them diminutive dik-diks threatened each other with two-inch-long horns, vying over territory. Often all three species could be found in one small clump of trees and bushes. The bushes where the giraffe and gerenuk fed looked like prize topiary specimens in an English garden, sculpted as they were by lips and tongues and teeth, without regard for the thorns.

Thomson's and Grant's gazelles in the thousands and impalas in like numbers fed, mated, produced their young, and virtually always died in the jaws or coils of predators. Rare indeed is the hoofed animal that dies of old age. Topi, kongoni, huge elands—the largest of all the world's antelopes, some weighing a half a ton—fed along with the rest. Warthogs, forever rushing around, were seldom out of view, folding their front legs under them as they stopped to feed in order to bring their mouths closer to their fodder. Zebras by the thousands,

Many kinds of antelopes and gazelles, like this gerenuk, with delicate legs and a long neck, gather in areas where there is plentiful food and water. ❖

white-bearded wildebeests by the tens of thousands, endless clusters of waterbucks, ostriches, bustards, fringe-eared oryx, pangolins, porcupines, honey badgers, and—wherever trees stood in clumps or stretched along riverbanks—monkeys, especially baboons in large numbers, were there. All of the different kinds of animals harvested, lived and died, and reacted to Ndovu as he did to them, with calculated indifference and the tolerance of a natural system in balance.

❖ ❖ ❖

It was near the large marsh at the center of the basin that Ndovu first encountered No Tusks. He was a young bull, almost two years younger than Ndovu, who was unusual among African elephants. He had no visible tusks and never would have. Otherwise he was a large, handsome animal who had been bullied in the sparring games in his own herd and had finally been driven away, not by cows intolerant of his growing maleness, but by the young bulls who gave him little peace.

Ndovu and No Tusks had been aware of each other for weeks. They smelled each other as their positions and the winds changed. Each mumbled and grumbled and made small screech sounds, perhaps to help each other keep track of a potential companion. There was no threat in any of it, and the two bulls began feeding closer and closer, until one morning during a brief but torrential downpour they came together and began feeding two feet apart, standing side by side, nose to tail. In that moment they touched, ran their trunks over each other, brushed against each other, and then shuffled off together to a deeper place in the marsh, and there all but submerged.

It was as simple as that. Ndovu would never be alone again except in his final hours of life, a time when all creatures are alone. No Tusks had become Ndovu's askari, a guard who would remain with him for as long as he lived. There would never be an opportunity for the askari to breed because he was tuskless. He would wait upon Ndovu when he covered cows, aroused by what he smelled and heard, but he would never challenge Ndovu or his own fate.

No Tusks was in reality Ndovu's new herd. With two great trunks searching the wind, with four weak, albeit forever searching, eyes, and with four enormously sensitive ears monitoring the area, each animal could relax a little more than had been possible when he had been alone. There was this sense of fulfillment too, the completeness that overtakes a herd animal when it has a herd. The familiar smell was always reassuring, providing a sense that everything was in place and well with the world.

In fact, though, all was not well. Without either animal knowing it, No Tusks was about to save Ndovu's life.

The men who hunt rhinoceroses' horns and elephants' ivory know the habitats these animals require for much of the year. Just as the other poachers had waited near the plateau while their scouts searched for them, other poachers knew well this basin with its ready water and rich feeding grounds. Three poachers working alone, without advance scouts, checked the area regularly. Elderly elephants, often carrying large tusks, would be likely to spend their final months in the vicinity of ready water and the pulpy water plants there.

Such elephants are the easiest targets of all. They are frequently alone, slower to react than peppery young cows and bulls, and so large that even the poorest marksman could hit the animal and bring it down.

Circling the marsh, the poachers picked up Ndovu's tracks and began following them with care. Winds over open water and along the channels of a marsh can be mischievous. Even a slight miscalculation could frighten a target elephant away.

Unlike trophy hunters who claim that hunting is a game, challenging their own wits against the superior natural senses and skills of an animal, the poachers engage in no foolish rationale. They want to kill as often and as easily as possible. They are neither gentlemen nor sportsmen and don't pretend to be. Like the mugger and the purse snatcher on a city street, the men who kill elephants for money have no false ego.

The three professional killers picked up Ndovu's tracks for the fourth straight morning, but on this day the wind was working for them. They could even smell the elephant, which was a good indication that if the breezes across the marsh held, the elephant would not smell them. They had never actually seen Ndovu, but his tracks were large and promised, or at least suggested, ample tusks. As they neared an extensive stand of papyrus, the wind did shift just slightly, and the papyrus parted. No Tusks was nearest the bank. He caught the scent of the invaders. Ndovu was almost a quarter of a mile away, out in the marsh, well hidden by a bunch of papyrus growing on a small island.

When the poachers saw No Tusks and realized there

was no profit in him, they fled. The wind had shifted again, and without being certain of where the men had gone, No Tusks was content to hold his ground, flap his ears, and bellow with rage. Out in the marsh, beyond the island, Ndovu answered. Later when the men encountered the tracks of two bulls, it would confirm that they had indeed heard a second elephant answer the first. But they decided against starting to stalk again. The bulls were young, alert, and vigorous. One had no ivory to offer at all, and the other was an unknown quantity. Besides, their working team had been reduced to two. The third man was still with them, but he had been rendered useless by a chance encounter, and in a day or two they would abandon him for the hyenas or lions to take.

When they had seen No Tusks, the three men had run away through an area of termite hills. On one of them was a six-foot-long, brick-red spitting cobra. It had whipped upright, opened its mouth wide, and contracted muscles just behind its jaw. Two venom sacs had been compressed, and the viscous yellow fluid was forced into two highly specialized fangs. Unlike normal venomous snake fangs that are shaped like a hypodermic needle, these fangs had round exit holes pointing forward halfway down. The venoms of the spitting cobras have finer molecular structures than the venoms of other snakes and when the red spitter's toxin shot forward from his gaping mouth, it broke into droplets until it was a force-driven mist. One of the three poachers was no more than three feet away from the termite hill when the snake, with unerring accuracy, reared and spit into the man's eyes. He reeled away in agony, covering his eyes with his hands and shouting for help. Eventually his partners circled back, and grabbing him by the upper arms, half dragged him away.

For a full day and a half they extended a strand of cloth for him to hold onto. But he was becoming burdensome and soon he would be left to die as, they knew, everything must. Had they taken him to water immediately after the encounter and flushed his eyes out for even a half an hour, he might not have lost his sight. As it was, he never regained it. The man was now hopelessly blind. The pain had been excruciating and the fear worse yet. He knew the inevitability of his fate. He would have done the same thing to any other human being on this earth except perhaps to his father. Mercy is not in the lexicon of the professional killer.

It had been luck again. If No Tusks had been farther out and Ndovu closer to shore, the poachers would have noted his tusks and persisted. They would have scattered and circled and waited until the wind was working for them again, and then they would have killed him.

About six weeks after Ndovu and No Tusks had established their bachelor herd, a third young bull worked around the edge of the marsh. They sensed him late one afternoon, but aside from a few throat sounds, did nothing to acknowledge him. Guardian, like No Tusks, was born to be a guard, and he was not threatening. Over a period of several days he fed closer and closer until the herd numbered three. Ndovu had his askaris, and they would always be near at hand. They would wander with him, feed and drink alongside him, join the herds he joined, and wait when he mated. They were a unit, now, with six ears, three trunks, and six not terribly useful eyes.

12

FIRST MATE

Ndovu, with Guardian and No Tusks in attendance, was feeding far out in the marsh in water that almost covered his back, when he first detected the great conglomerate herd approaching. He could hear their increasingly loud  shrilling sounds. As with the bad, dry time when Ndovu was very young but had still been able to make the journey to the river, a number of herds had come together, driven by drought to seek water and food far from their usual range. Sandstorms over the Sahara Desert, far to the north and beyond the mountains, had launched tropical storms in the South Atlantic, and at the same time had diverted desperately needed moisture from over vast areas of East and Central Africa. Far out in the Indian Ocean on the island of Sri Lanka, another species of elephant was being deluged by unseasonable monsoonlike storms of ferocious intensity. But the land surrounding Ndovu's marsh was drying up.

The upper atmosphere was in turmoil, and vast numbers of animals far below the hurricane-force air currents suffered the consequences when the rains failed. During such periods of drought, some creatures simply withdraw into themselves, some stop reproducing, some enter a form of suspended animation, some fish and amphibians encase themselves in mud to wait out the drought, and plant seeds settle into temporary, though extended, dormancy. Organisms as complex as elephants can do none of these things. They must wander until enough water is found.

Somehow the huge herd had sensed the impending catastrophe far in advance and had begun the trek well before the rains failed. The land funneled the animals toward this basin, and once in it they were naturally brought together around the edges of the great marsh. They came from all points of the compass in twos and threes, in dozens, and by the score. They came thirsty and hungry and covered with dust. Swarms of biting insects followed them and buzzed over them in blankets because they had not had the tons of mud needed to cover themselves for weeks, and sand tossed back over their shoulders offered little protection. They were parched and exhausted, and every now and then one would stumble. Most managed to recover, drawn onward by the smell of water, which was richer and more beckoning with every step they took. Even in their anxiety they did not forget the core of the herd, the calves. The young were watched and guided and protected from dangers that were more often imagined than real, if elephants can be said to imagine anything.

In all, well over five hundred elephants had been on their way toward the marsh for weeks. Dozens had been lost along the march. Most of the elephants who were five years old or older had been to the basin before at least once, and many of them had made the trek repeatedly. And although the richness of the place had saved them, by offering food and water in the huge quantities they required, they had always moved away after every visit.

Elephants move on even from nearly perfect habitats. Otherwise they would all congregate in a few small places and in time would render these places useless and themselves extinct. No habitat can tolerate a really large elephant population indefinitely. Elephants must have places in reserve, however, where they can go in emergencies.

The hundreds of elephants Ndovu first heard and then smelled coming toward the water would do enormous damage. The bankside papyrus would be crushed and nearby trees would be uprooted and knocked over or debarked.

The shape of the pond and the marsh banks would be altered by a parade of giant feet. Grass clumps would vanish, be eaten or crushed by the endless shuffling, and by the time the herd splintered and dispersed, the winds that blew across the marsh's open water leads would create small dust storms as soon as they touched land. Dust devils would gyrate and cavort like small tornados, as many as twenty at a time. Five hundred elephants are capable of converting an area of even very dense forests into a treeless grass savannah in a few

Elephants seem to sense an impending dry period and begin to march toward new sources of water long before the drought begins. ❖

years. Anything as fragile as a marsh system can begin to alter and lose its organic shape in a matter of hours, once an invasion begins.

Great changes involving both plants and animals and even local weather patterns near the surface of the earth can occur within weeks. Dust changes the color of the sky, and sunrises and sunsets become more spectacular. Gold and red are suffused with amazing shades of burnt umber, purple, green, blue, orange, and the red of flames and lava. The land glows, and elephants seem iridescent. And above that, thunder rolls and there are faint horizontal flashes—lightning strobing through the immodest color show—but still the rain does not fall.

The elephants who were now on their way would eventually disperse. A few of the very old animals would stay on to die alone, but the main body of the huge congregation would leave as soon as the young and the old who could still travel were sufficiently refreshed. In each case it would be a senior cow who would give the orders for her unit to move on. When young were born to a herd in the area of the marsh, the whole herd would stay a few days longer to give the infants a chance to gain strength and become established as members of the group.

When the great gathering did come apart, though, it would be because the weather had broken elsewhere. The high altitude wind shifts would have played out, and the earth and the sky would once again be in equilibrium. There would be rain, and once again there would be surface water.

There is enormous vitality to a marsh because of the almost limitless numbers of individual plants and animals that constitute its whole. So, although great damage can be done by such an invasion as Ndovu was witnessing, it would all be repaired or replaced. Downed or dying trees might take decades, and in some cases centuries, to be replaced, but the seeds were in place and the nurturing earth rich in dung. The slaughtered trees themselves would become gardens, providing miniuniverses along their downed lengths for an incredible variety of life. Not a fiber would be lost, all of their parts were organic and would be consumed in an inexorable process by everything from bacteria to insect larvae. Thigmotactic creatures—that is insects and other arthropods, animals that burrow into decay because the peculiar tropistic reactions of their bodies demand that they be touched on all sides simultaneously—would find the fallen trees and create networks in them. Birds would help pull the rotting masses apart even faster as they hopped and hunted along their lengths for the burrowers and the crawlers. Reptiles would find cover from the sun and their predators, and small mammals would hide there too and sometimes die in coils or from injected digestive enzymes called venom.

The visiting elephants would add many tons of dung to the nutrients already being spread across the area every day by the other species. Smaller plants, grasses, papyrus included, and fungi would all spring back and in some places increase their vitality at least for a while because their competition had been crushed or consumed by the foraging elephants.

While the elephants were in the area, the greatest of the local predators would have to move away. There were too many elephants who were nervous about their young to allow the lions any sleep at all. Cats may sleep

Foraging elephants wreak havoc on an area, crushing plants and grass, but adding nutrients to the soil in the form of tons of dung. ❖

up to eighteen or even nineteen hours a day. With five hundred or so very pushy elephants in the vicinity, the local lions could not get any rest at all. No sooner would a couple of bachelors or a pride of mothers with young settle down to sleep off a gluttonous feast, than there would be a shrill blast of alarm, and a phalanx of angry elephants—ears spread wide, trunks thrust forward— would begin shuffling in on them at twenty-five to thirty miles an hour. A lion can hide his tough, tawny body in appropriate vegetation, but never his scent—not from anxious elephants. And with new young being born every day, the elephants were nervous to the point of aggression, particularly toward predators they knew would take a calf, if possible. Very few elephant calves are actually taken by lions, but elephants treat lions as if this were an everyday possibility.

The lions would scatter—occasionally a very young cub would be momentarily forgotten and get left behind. He would be picked up by an elephant cow and flicked out into the marsh where he would drown. But no matter how quickly the cats gave ground, it would be only a matter of minutes before more elephants repeated the display and drove them off again. Often stopping to look back over their shoulders and glower with apparent disgust and with as much disdain as they could muster, the lions moved off and took refuge in some low hills and tight, narrow valleys a full dozen miles away. Aggregations that had come together because of the richness of the place would disassemble just as the elephants would soon do, and a casual feeding association of thirty or more lions would quickly become small, fairly tight-knit groups of two to six or seven animals.

Lions scatter when elephants are in the vicinity. ❖

There were plenty of hoofed animals even that far from the water, and others were constantly arriving because of the drought now spreading over an area of thousands of square miles. More and more the marsh was becoming an oasis. Even some of the smaller ponds in the great, lush basin were drying up as the streams that fed them with water from the hills and underground springs began to fail. Cats don't like being pushed off their turf, but they had no choice. The largest of them would either give way or die. With new calves being born every day, the elephants had declared the marsh a lion-free zone, and there was no way the lions could safely contest the decision. No species but man ever can.

Two leopards also decided to move away for as long as the elephants were in the vicinity. Actually, since it was a mother and her daughter, the decision was made by the older cat who was as worried about her offspring as the elephants were about theirs. The two spotted cats moved even farther away, for there were too many lions in the low hills. A lion will steal a leopard's cub while several other members of the pride haze the enraged adult. But, then, hyenas do the same thing to lions. And if the necessity arises, a leopard or a lion will kill young hyenas if the adults are too wily to allow themselves to be taken.

When it came to parenting, the lions seemed more casual then either the leopards or the elephants. In fact, in one of the smaller hideaways in the hills where the lions took refuge, a female was inattentive for just a few moments, something an elephant mother would rarely be, and that was long enough for the male with whom she had mated a few months earlier to move in and kill three of his own cubs outright. The fourth was so badly mangled, he would die in a few hours. The female attacked the male, and then a bachelor who had been traveling with the infanticidal male attacked the female. It all ended up with relatively little adult blood being spilled, but a great deal of alarm and commotion. When a lot of elephants come into an area, they cause a great deal of noise and confusion among the resident species, even though they might be relatively quiet and peaceful themselves.

Inevitably there were females ready to breed in the great gathering, and Ndovu was ready for that stage of his life to begin. A clock had been ticking since the moment of his birth, and now the hour had struck.

Ndovu was a commanding bull with enormous mass and huge tusks. He came up out of the marsh as the first elephants started to arrive, and stood watchful, sensing more with his ears and his nervously twisting and coiling trunk than with his eyes.

He stood at the edge of the marsh looking black except for a gray stripe along his spine where the water had not quite covered him. Yellow-billed oxpeckers perched on each of his tusks, and one sat in the center of his sloping forehead. He tolerated the birds flitting around his face and body because they rid him of external parasites. Red-billed oxpeckers did the same chore, and slightly to the west the task went to small black birds known as piapiacks. Ndovu's trunk moved left and right in search of clues, and he flapped his ears. He moved restlessly in a semiaroused state in anticipation of a new element in his life.

Ndovu quickly began moving toward a small cluster of seven cows with two very young calves and two juveniles. It was a microcosm of a herd within the growing assembly. But unlike the larger herd and subherds, these were animals that had bonded and their bond carried promise. Among the others was a cow whose bull calf was eight years old and who was now frequently wandering off on his own. The cow was again ready to mate. Ndovu's odor changed as his interest increased, and the receptive cow easily identified him. How elephants are attracted to each other is not really understood. There is a way, though, for females must choose correctly if the power and vitality of the species is to be sustained.

After the herd members had bathed and consumed enough water between them to create a not so terribly small pond of their own, they moved off to explore the different food opportunities that the lush area provided. Ndovu followed at a discreet distance with No Tusks and Guardian in attendance.

At times Ndovu was as much as a mile behind the herd of cows and their young, but the cow in estrus knew he was there and fell to the rear of the line of march. The cows moved from one feeding opportunity to another, as if the dry fodder that had barely sustained them during their trek left them anxious to try everything green again that they had ever known in other good times of rain and flowing rivers.

Toward dawn, while the air was still cool, Ndovu caught up with the female. No Tusks and Guardian moved in close to the other cows and began to feed with them. They were inspected and accepted. They were not the challenging kind.

Ndovu moved directly to the cow's side and began to caress her with his trunk, and then used it to explore the area between her hind legs. He brushed against her, making a rough sandy sound as their hides abraded, and he caressed her some more before placing the tip of his trunk in her mouth. She did the same with her trunk, and they stood joined in that way for several minutes. In some strange way there was a poetry to their pose, a great gray gentleness that expressed the wonder and the beauty of life in eternal replication. They were quiet with each other, even tender, or so at least human beings would perceive it. It was an intense but orderly process, and their genes told them what to do as stimulation flowed from one to the other and then back again, enhanced.

Ndovu moved around behind his mate-to-be and made a perfunctory effort to mount her, but quickly slipped back down to all four feet again. She then initiated a mock chase of sorts, and he played along because she was not seriously trying to avoid him.

When she stopped and faced him, he gently rocked, pressing his face against hers, and there were several more minutes of trunk play. The sounds they made, the sweet nothings of our species, were soft and low and lacked threat or violence as did all of their foreplay. The growing intensity would make both of them ready to contribute their maximum in the union that followed.

And then it was time. Ndovu and First Mate knew it at the same time. He went around behind her, prodded her in the rump with his tusks, and then assumed an almost sitting position. He rose to an almost standing position to accomplish intromission, and his forelegs lay along either side of her spine. In a hundred seconds it was over, and Ndovu slipped off the cow, bumping his chest on her rump as he went down to a normal stance. The two began browsing near each other, and again, forty minutes later, the latter part of the sequence was repeated. Just before actual sunrise, Ndovu mounted First Mate for a third time, and then withdrew to stand alone and rest.

For as long as the herd remained at the marsh, Ndovu, No Tusks, and Guardian remained with them. They respected the position of the senior cow and offered no threat either to the young or the herd's tranquility. On one occasion Ndovu was attracted by the scent of another cow in estrus in another herd just down channel from where he and his adopted herd were drinking and wallowing. He investigated but found the cow in the company of a mature, experienced bull his own size with just slightly smaller tusks. He decided against making the challenge and returned to his own new group and mounted First Mate briefly without successful intromission. He moved out into deeper water and moved his head back and forth quickly, creating swirls and currents with his trunk. Then he rolled over on his side until he was covered with water, the tip of his trunk alone periscoping, seeking air.

❖ ❖ ❖

First Mate stood looking out over the water. No Tusks and Guardian fed alongside the other cows. Their young fed nearby, two infants nursed, and in the distance insistent thunder and lightning pointed earthward and foretold the changes that would take the huge conglomeration of elephants away from the marsh. During the time of the great invasion, though, Ndovu had been able to stamp his first mark on the future. There would be many more to assure him of immortality.

13

THE STALK

When several weeks had passed and First Mate's herd began wandering farther from the marsh, Ndovu, No Tusks, and Guardian stayed with it. They trailed along behind, but always close enough so that when the herd stopped to  forage, drink, or bathe, the three bulls were quickly among them, blending in easily. On sev-eral occasions the herd stayed away from the marsh for one whole day and night, but still returned to har-vest the succulent waterside vegetation and to bathe and indulge in hour-long drinking and water-blowing sprees.

Under the leadership of Auntie, a huge old cow, the herd constantly tested the wind. Someday many of them would be back. Now, though, the time had come to leave. A restlessness moved through the group and all the animals felt it; it took only the signal of their leader to start the trek.

Auntie manipulated and commanded her small group, but with their acquiescence. She didn't punish or even really threaten except when young bulls behaved roughly around the very young. Then she could be ominous. She led the herd by a silent consensus, and the other cows were comfortable following her. She was wise in the way of elephants, and her decisions had been good for the herd. When that was no longer true, the herd would not heed her signals and would no longer follow her.

But the elephants as a group needed structure. They had to follow a senior animal, and Auntie had come through experience and a naturally commanding nature to be that leader. With her own young and those of other cows, she was a great nurturer. Elephants, like human beings, produce natural leaders.

Ndovu and his attending guards were comfortable with her too. For them, their wandering as bachelors had allowed them time to mature. Ndovu was much larger than Auntie, more agile, much faster, and potentially far more aggressive. Still, he would not challenge Auntie or create unease among the cows and their young. If danger threatened the herd, if lions were detected nearby, he would act the bull, that certainly. But it was Auntie who led the way, selected the trails through the hills, determined how long her followers should spend in any one area to feed, to drink, and to bathe. She was the first to move down a riverbank, the first to enter the water. While the other cows, and now the three males traveling with them, ate or rested, drank and flopped over in the water, Auntie listened and

The female elephant that leads the herd must be able to discipline the fractious young bulls, as well as make the decisions that will benefit the whole group. ❖

tested the air endlessly with her restless trunk. The rest of the herd listened to her. Her suspicion was their suspicion, her unrest was theirs. And she had always been the lead when a young bull had to be sent away from the herd.

First Mate had passed through her estrus and had conceived. A fetus was forming inside her uterus. A single egg had been invaded by one of Ndovu's sperm. After sealing itself off from further intrusions, it quickly became two cells, then four, then eight, and continued to double until now it was implanted in First Mate's uterine wall as a very tiny elephant. First Mate would not be ready to breed again for four or five years and even then might not be receptive to advances from bulls who would approach her.

The small herd now wandered eastward from the marsh. Rain had fallen over a broad area and within days everything was green. The open areas were pocked by millions of wildflowers ranging from the size of a human fist to almost microscopic. Young animals safely beyond infancy appeared from underground burrows, and birds laid their eggs and incubated them in nests located everywhere, from hidden positions on the ground to high places in the tallest trees. It was a fresh, clean time, dust was held to a minimum, and grass spread out and grew taller every hour. Seed pods ripened and burst, and pollen floated on every draft of air. The wondrous fertility and resilience of the African land had been released by the addition of that single substance, water. Everything that lived, the elephants included, waited upon its arrival to resume their lives.

Some animals lived their entire lives within the compass of a few thousand square yards, some in even less space than that. The elephants, greatest of the terrestrial nomads, needed thousands of square miles.

Auntie's group may or may not have had an actual destination. They wandered, and until water again became a priority, their path seemed a random one. Equally mysterious was the length of time the herd spent in one place. An area with relatively sparse vegetation might hold their attention for several days, so long as drinking and bathing water was in good supply. Another area, far richer in all things good for elephants, might hold their attention for a day or less.

One day they would work assiduously to clear an area of lions, and the next day they might avoid another place because of the pervasive odor of lion urine. One area they skirted was the home hunting range of one of the few large packs of cape hunting dogs left in East Africa. There had been an outbreak of distemper, and many of the dogs had died. Nothing had eaten them except for some perfunctory picking by a dozen or so Egyptian vultures, and the remains lay scattered over a couple of square miles. Auntie led her herd around and then away from the area of pestilence.

A month after leaving the marsh behind, Ndovu with his guardian bulls was still with the cows and the young being led by the ever-watchful Auntie. Ndovu paid no more attention to First Mate than he did to any of the other cows. Sex is in the soul of the elephant, but poetry is not. Gentleness had been part of the ritual for Ndovu, as big and potentially dangerous as he was, because it was a functional prelude to the actual coupling, but the sequence leading up to conception had been without any of the romance of which human beings sing.

Six weeks into their wanderings the small herd was missing Guardian. They had crossed a trail of another herd late one afternoon, and by chance had encountered an area where a female in full heat had urinated copiously. Ndovu showed no interest, and No Tusks was too attached to Ndovu to leave him. The cows detected the scent mark as readily as the bulls did and circled the spot in seeming agitation. When at last the herd moved on, they left Guardian standing there looking after them. Then he turned and trudged purposefully on his own.

Guardian would soon find the cow in estrus, but she was already taken by a larger, more aggressive bull. He would wait several days on the edges of this new herd, and then the cow would let him cover her, although she had already conceived and it was a futile exercise.

❖ ❖ ❖

But there was eventual purpose to it all. Guardian would stay on with his new herd, which was led by an ancient cow, Aged. The dominant bull who had possessed the cow whose trail Guardian had followed would leave after a few weeks and link up briefly with yet another herd. Thus do bulls wander in and out of the lives of cow herds with their young. Some bulls linger on with a particular group of cows for as much as a year or more, but their attachments are generally more ephemeral than that. When another cow in the herd Guardian had joined came into heat a month later, he would impregnate her.

❖ ❖ ❖

The movement of the small elephant herds in the great valley was known to the men who love ivory but not the natural bearers of the precious substance. Men came into the valley, dug up rolled animal hides that had been buried in certain places, and from those putrid bundles they lifted out automatic rifles and waxed boxes of cartridges. The arms had been put in prearranged spots by army patrols, on orders from high-placed politicians and generals.

The hired killers, most of them from Somalia itself or the Somali tribe inside Kenya's northern border, cleaning their freshly exhumed arms, began the hunt with a purpose. They knew their quarry well enough so that a careless move, an ill-timed advance that ignored the wind, could drive the herds so far away it would take them weeks to get back into the position again. Wily elephants, many people believe, are the only ones to have survived the recent slaughter. They say that elephants and rhinoceroses both are now selectively breeding for man-fear. Only those individual animals hypersensitive to and fearful of the scent of man live long enough to breed often. More trusting animals are naturally the easiest to stalk and the first to die.

The killers knew well how much hard work would have to follow the slaughter. The heavy tusks would have to be hacked from the elephants' faces with pangas and axes and then be carried sometimes twenty or thirty miles or more, to be wrapped in fresh hides and buried, again in prearranged places. Other men with trucks or helicopters would dig up the tusks weeks later and lift them away to Mombasa for transport to Tokyo and Hong Kong. It was all arranged by men with access to fax machines and secured telephone lines.

The first trail the men encountered after securing their arms was the one laid down by Auntie and her group. Ndovu, No Tusks, and a newly appended third and smaller bull were the only males. There were now eleven cows, four young animals, and four infants. The herd was on the move because it had not rained for over two and a half weeks, and the fragile surface water system was beginning to show the effects. Auntie's herd was averaging only a few hours at the lesser water holes and thinner rivers and then moving on. The infants were tiring, but were nowhere near ready to give out yet. The herd was pushing on, but it was still far from being a panicky flight.

The killers had the herd in sight several times, but they held back until it was moving over more broken ground. Using great care it is possible to stalk elephants on flat land, but it takes exquisite attention to the wind, agonizingly slow movement, and very often a great deal of travel on hands and knees. It is much easier to make a mistake out in the open.

In a small valley, the men spotted Auntie's herd moving toward a wooded area of mixed acacia, yellow fever trees, and other greater and lesser growth. It was late in the day, and the men had already watched the herd at a narrow river an hour before. The prize was theirs. The elephants would spend the night among the trees and at first light, emerge and almost certainly continue the line of march they had been following for three days. That would be the killing ground. The men would circle the valley and the two hills that formed its saddle and be in position when the elephants appeared at dawn. They had already made note of Ndovu's worth and the third bull, Crasher, had reasonable tusks as well. Four of the cows also carried substantial ivory by today's reduced standards.

The killing would take less than ten minutes. Extracting the ivory would be done in about an hour and a half, and the planned burial site was now only about a dozen miles to the east. The men could then begin positioning themselves on another herd by midafternoon, if all went well. In a little less than a week they could harvest just about all of the valley's ivory. They suspected that there were two rhinoceroses in the area, and they intended to be on the lookout for them too. It promised to be a good week, even if a little bit tiring, if everything worked out as they had planned.

As the men predicted, Auntie and her followers did spend the night in the wooded area, and at least most of her followers stayed with her. There had been no cow in heat for over a month, and Ndovu was restless. About the time the moon moved around the farthest hill and the shadows deepened, Ndovu, followed closely by No Tusks, began to move away. Beyond the edge of the trees there was a small erratic movement of air, and it bore the two odors Ndovu both hated and feared the most. There was the pungency of man and the sickening sweetness of gun oil. Ndovu was aware of them at once and moved away swiftly with No Tusks hurrying to keep up. At sunup they were nearly twenty miles away and still moving.

Also at sunup Auntie and her followers, the third bull, her cows and young moved out of the trees in the direction of the water they had detected at a distance the night before. The men had guessed correctly, it was on the herd's line of march.

Auntie, with all of her elephant wisdom locked up inside her, was the first to die. A stream of bullets, each one impacting an inch above the one before it, climbed from her lower jaw, across her face, and into her brain case. She fell onto her far side and died with her legs kicking futilely out to the side. The other cows, the third bull, and even two of the young with only little bud tusks to show for their years died too.

If the men had cared about elephants even a little, they would have shot all of the young as well. Terrified, confused, and doomed, they were driven away by the men who saved their bullets rather than offer even a small measure of mercy. Lions sleeping on a slope nearby fled to the far side of the hill when the gunfire erupted. Slowly, hearing the young elephants and the infants making their alarm and fear sounds, the cats worked their way up over the hill again and watched with interest until the men were done, until they had shouldered their ivory and rifles and started to move away.

It isn't easy for a lion to kill even a young elephant because they are so chunky. There is no exposed throat to grab, no windpipe to crush that lions can get at. The head does not easily bend back nor is the neck easy to break. But given time, lions can pull young elephants to the ground and slowly kill them. At least that is so when several lions are acting in concert.

14

THE EARTH
SPEAKS

All through the day that Auntie died, and the night that followed, Ndovu, with No Tusks trailing a few feet behind, moved away from the area of the dreaded scents. They traveled eastward, facing the gold and red of the morning  that was forming beyond the great escarpment that surrounded the valley.

The valley itself, known as the Great Rift Valley, is the greatest geological feature on the earth except for the ocean basins. Computer-enhanced photographic images taken by orbiting satellites show it slashing its way across the face of the planet.

Extending from Syria in the northeast to Southwest Africa, the Great Rift Valley is still being formed. It has been in the making for millions of years, but is still very young in geological time. In the valley are volcanoes, now quiet but recently with active flows of lava calderas, or silent volcano throats, large and small, geysers, and areas of intense geothermal activity. There are hills, some freshly made and sharp-edged, others older and now rounded into gentle knolls. There are also vast lakes, countless rivers, marshes, and streams, arid areas, forests, all contained within the valley's high walls, along with some of the largest concentrations of animals left on this planet. Within this area the Pleistocene Age lives on. It is a place of wild biological drama, an unrelenting zoological passion play. The elephant is only one of the species that flourishes here.

The two badly frightened bulls did not stop to eat for more than a few minutes at a time. Ndovu's intense fear was the product of his experiences as a younger animal, first high on the plateau and then on the outskirts of the village near the electrified fence. For his sensitive ears, the explosions close at hand were shattering. And no animal likes surprises, for in nature, surprise frequently equates with death, or at the very least pain, and hence the lifesaving fear. Fear and pain are actually gifts of nature.

Ndovu had been able to identify the two scent signals that warned him. No Tusks had no such experiences in his life to teach him directly about the man-smell and the smell of gun oil, but Ndovu's fear communicated itself clearly, and so tightly bonded had the two bulls become that the emotions of one quickly became the reactions of the other. They were a social unit and now functioned best when close to each other. No Tusks did not need a mate, but he needed another of his kind to belong to. Ndovu needed and would take mates readily, but they were always temporary, whereas the faithful No Tusks was a permanent bond.

Neither Ndovu nor No Tusks knew that Auntie and her entire herd were dead. They had been well away by the time of the massacre.

The infant elephants that the poachers had left alive were already half consumed by lions. Predictably, troops of hyenas were arriving at the scene. Over two hundred and fifty vultures had massed overhead. They had covered the arena of death squawking loudly. With the dead young and adult elephants lying over an area of half a square mile, there were enormous quantities of flesh for the predators and the scavengers to consume. By sunup the process was well underway.

The poachers had profited little from the merciless carnage they had wrought. Their heavy barrage of gunfire had attracted a larger than usual antipoaching patrol, alerted in advance by villagers who had been enlisted in an intelligence network. The poachers had come into the tiny village seeking beer and women. Their rough manner and their out-country accents had marked them, as did the freely flowing coins they spread around.

The villagers hated poachers because they belonged to an alien tribe and took whatever livestock they wanted. Worse yet, they attracted patrols and government attention, which no village wants because the villagers themselves are always under a cloud, always suspect. They do, after all, harvest some smaller wildlife for their own use, and that is illegal too. In Africa anonymity is a safe and reassuring thing. It is simply better if the poachers do not come. Their arrogance has bought them no friends, and for the villagers they are trade goods; they can be bartered for money.

A runner, who was as wise in the ways of the wild as the poachers themselves were, left in the night and found the patrol and alerted them. That patrol had radioed a second unit to join them for a possible major encounter. They linked up in time to hear the dawn gunfire that wiped out Auntie and her herd. They knew that they had arrived too late to save one elephant herd, but in time to end the marauders' careers.

The runner from the village had taken them to the place where other ivory had already been buried, for there are no secrets in Africa. The runner was paid and he left, anxious to get back to his village. It was, after all, not his fight. The patrol rightly guessed the poachers would bring their latest harvest to the same burial site, and they took up positions on the hills near the hiding place.

In a few hours the poachers arrived, carrying both the guns and the ivory. The patrol had orders to take at least one prisoner from this encounter for interrogation, and it had been agreed that the last man in the line (for the gang was certain to be walking single file) would be shot in the legs only, to keep him from running away.

Once again, since the patrol was badly outgunned by the poachers' automatic weapons, surprise was essential. If given an opportunity, the poachers would open fire and the members of the patrol would be singled out, hunted down, and killed. It was possible that the village would be punished too. The poachers function best when terror rules.

The senior patrol leader fired first, and the poachers with their heavy loads fell dead simultaneously as the hills rang with reverberations and the rifles had their say. When the men of the patrol clamored down from the rocks where their ambush positions had been set, they found that the last man, who was meant to be kept alive, had taken one of the three shots that hit him through the femoral artery. He was almost dead by the time the men reached him. Within another minute and a half he had bled to death. The poachers' guns were collected and the ivory stacked, while the hoards already buried from previous slaughters were exhumed. The runner who had gone back to his village had gone first to the district commissioner's house. There was a radio there, and the message went out. Two trucks were on the way and would go by the village and pick up the runner at dawn. He would guide them to the graveyard of elephant tusks, the patrol guarding it, and to the dead poachers.

The ivory, almost six tons of it all together, and the poachers' automatic rifles were loaded aboard the trucks, and then the patrol climbed on top of them for the trip out and a week's rest in the market town of Ragoma. The paramilitary unit would then resume its endless marches, looking for clues as to other poachers' movements, while waiting for news from the informers' network. The bodies of the poachers were placed in a neat line, their pockets emptied of coins, and then they were left to the fate of all animals that die out on the African land. Their fate would be the same as that of the elephants a dozen miles away. In nature there is no reason at all why distinctions should be drawn. In fact, none exist.

❖ ❖ ❖

Ndovu and No Tusks had reached an area of sparsely placed but ample fruit-bearing trees. It had good grass and a narrow but well-supplied river.

The two bulls stayed in the area of the river for several days. Food was both diverse and plentiful. Only two incidents occurred to punctuate their hours. Two lions attempted to approach the river, but Ndovu and No Tusks drove them off, allowing them no dignity at all. Exercising the elephant's prerogative to choose its neighbors, the two bulls engaged in a little recreational bullying. There were no calves around, and the two young lions were certainly no threat to the adult bulls, but elephants seem to enjoy that kind of thing and the thoroughly disgruntled lions left without drinking. They had never even reached the water before being turned away.

The second minor recreation centered on an enormous iridescent python. It was nineteen feet long and was digesting a young impala it had eaten two days before. It was stretched out between two fallen trees, the victims of other elephants that had visited the river several months before. Ndovu caught the scent of the snake and managed to get it by the tail and drag it out of hiding. Before it could strike and deliver its damaging but nonvenomous bite, Ndovu stepped on its back, and then did it again and again. The snake was crushed and its back broken wherever Ndovu stepped. Ndovu worried the snake for several minutes after it was dead because it kept coiling convulsively, as it would do for at least another two hours from nerve reflexes.

Eventually Ndovu left his victim and entered the river and grumbled softly to himself. No Tusks moved over to watch the snake for a few minutes, then joined Ndovu in the river. It was a relatively quiet time and small diversions were welcome.

Several days after Ndovu and No Tusks arrived at the Edenlike riverside area, a small herd of seven cows with four babies and two barely mature bulls joined them. The arriving herd hung back among the trees when it sensed the presence of the strange bulls. After several minutes the lead cow, Trekker, came out of the trees and paraded up and down with her trunk partially extended and arched. Her tail stuck out straight behind her. When Ndovu, in a ceremonial gesture, turned away and stepped down into the river, Trekker relaxed and followed him. Her herd followed suit. It was no more complicated than that.

Ndovu and his companion mixed with the new group easily and when it left after two days of feeding and drinking, Ndovu and No Tusks went with it.

The animals moved toward the south only four miles west of the Rift Valley's eastern slopes. There was good food and water along the way, so the herd's movement had the feeling of drifting rather than trekking.

The new course that Ndovu, No Tusks, and their latest adopted herd took led them through a variety of landscapes and habitats. They ate, bathed, drank, and occasionally chased off lions.

A hundred yards from a small pond, the herd stopped to inspect a freshly used mud wallow that reeked unmistakably of black rhinoceros, one of a pitiful remnant still left in the area. These giants also once numbered in the hundreds of thousands (in the case of elephants, however, the number was a good many millions), but poaching began affecting the rhinoceroses earlier and more intensely than it has even the elephants.

Of Africa's two species of rhinoceroses, the so-called black and the white, the latter is much the larger of the two. Both are the same color, a shade of gray that looks black only when the animals are wet or freshly muck-covered from a good roll in a wallow. The black rhinoceros, the kind Ndovu was about to encounter, is more accurately called the prehensile-lipped rhino, for its upper lip functions as a kind of thumb in eating. That lip is to this species of rhinoceros what a trunk is to the elephant, although it is nowhere near as long, nor as versatile or powerful. It is like a finger compared to an arm.

The other species, the white, has a broad upper lip that is distinctly different. The species always was less common in East Africa than it was in the southern part of the continent (it is gone from East Africa now, totally wiped out), and "white" is the Boer pronunciation of the English word "wide." The white rhino is the wide-lipped or square-lipped rhino.

The herd now came to the pond and stood facing a large female black rhinoceros and her calf. It was an easy standoff. Neither species was predatory, and they could readily coexist for a day or two or even a year. One of the young bulls, however, had to play his role as a macho teenager and moved around the pond and squared off with the female. Several factors were at play. The rhinoceros's eyesight is no better than the elephant's, and the cow did have a calf to protect. Although by no means a herd animal, rhinoceroses are very concerned for the safety of their young.

As soon as the cow could determine what the young bull was doing, actually threatening her right to use the pond, she squared off, waited a few moments, and then charged. Her head was down, her long front horn was ready to hook upward into the throat or side of her tormentor. She was amazingly agile and once she had made up her mind, she was very determined. The young elephant bull squealed in alarm and fled the field of battle without the two animals even coming close to each other.

Now, however, a young member of the herd had been alarmed. It didn't matter that his behavior had contributed to the situation. The herd was immediately involved. With Trekker in the lead, the herd moved around the pond ominously, absorbing the fleeing young bull back into their midst as they went. The cow rhinoceros, with her young calf very close to her side, moved off into some deep grass, snuffling and snorting as she went, her tail sticking up and her chin elevated as well. The elephants were satisfied to parade around the pond, trumpeting to relieve their tension, and then they went into the water and took a communal bath. Later that evening the rhinoceros and her calf returned and drank not far from where the elephants stood grazing. At the sight of them the pesky young bull hid behind his mother, and there were no further encounters.

The animals had all done what was required of them. The stubborn, protective, potentially aggressive rhinoceros mother had mock-charged in response to a threat from an immature elephant bull. The elephants had immediately mock-charged the rhinoceros in response to *her* response, in a show of solidarity. Most animals, in fact, would much rather display than fight. It is just as satisfying in the end and a great deal less bloody.

One morning just after the plovers and the sand-grouse began scolding the sun, and the owls had settled in next to thick tree trunks and begun to wink and blink, there was a sudden and at first unidentifiable blur. The sun seemed to be in two places at the same time, trees inexplicably seemed to have two trunks, and then the hills seemed to move.

There was a pause, and then the trees snapped sidewise like drunken things. Many toppled over and pitched down hillsides, swallowed up in cascades of collapsing rock formations and sliding layers of earth. The sideways jolt was like a monstrous slap on the head. No Tusks fell over onto his side and struggled to get himself upright again. Ndovu managed to stay on his feet but only barely. Trekker turned to flee, although there was no place to go, and she went to her knees. The younger elephants squealed in terror.

The trail through the hills that the herd had just used vanished as two hillsides poured down, then flowed out onto flat land. A cow and her calf who had been slow in moving out with the herd were buried, and their sounds of terror went unheard, smothered in the screaming and roaring of the landscape adjustments. The surface of the earth itself was grinding, and the noise was enormous.

The earthquake's second shock wave hit thirty-nine seconds after the first, and then there was a full sixty seconds of quiet, deep in the earth, before the largest jolt of all shifted land sideways and cracked open the bottom of a lake nearby. Its entire contents vanished into the crack and poured far below onto another sea, this one of molten rock reeking with sulfurous gas that would have killed anything that had not been consumed by the heat.

For a moment there was a badly creased sea of mud. Then a fierce, giant gush of steam—with fish, amphibians, and twenty-three hippopotamuses equally distributed through the geyser of vaporized lake, equally cooked and torn apart in seconds—jetted to the sky. In its wake, waterfowl that had been too slow to respond were sucked down into the lake bed and transformed as well.

Ancient rock formations inside the hills split apart and laid bare fossils not of life but of time, for they had cooled in place eons ago before there was life on earth. Trekker, one other cow, one of the young bulls, one female calf, Ndovu, and No Tusks were the only members of the herd to survive. The jolt had been so severe that men and women a hundred and fifty miles away had been thrown off their feet, and three hundred miles away cattle lowed and sheep bleated in disquiet and fear.

The place where Ndovu and his companions were gathering for their morning bath and drink had been almost directly over the site where far below, two adjacent mountain-sized blocks of tectonic plate had snapped. One plate had plunged over the other for a dozen feet, sending thundering waves on ahead, tearing through softer crustal structures, shattering or displacing formations that weighed millions of tons. It was like the cracking of a giant whip by the time the stunning shock waves reached the earth's surface, as if all of the twist and the torque that had brought the great valley into being had been released at once.

The number of animals that died cannot be imagined. Fifty miles away hundreds of colonial weaverbird nests fell to the ground with their helpless young inside. Termite hills thirty and forty feet deep folded inward, trapping and crushing tenanting reptiles. The shearing action of the earth cut many in half as neatly as if it had been done with a great knife. Hoofed animals aborted, others were buried, and many suffered broken legs and had their fate quickly sealed. What would have come to them all eventually would now come to them in hours or days at the most. The cascading soil and rockslides carried a vast assortment of living creatures to their doom. Tortoises had their shells cracked open like coconuts, and mothers of all kinds lost their young.

The thunder that rolled through the earth, echoing the birth of continents, awoke monsters that slept beneath huge craters that had been in place for hundreds of thousands of years. Some of those volcanoes would rumble back into life in the months and years ahead. The ferocity of the shock had been just shy of the force needed to cast up and pull down whole mountains.

It had been the kind of cataclysmic event that dinosaurs knew, and now Ndovu knew too. Once again he walked out of the storm, and although the dust thrown up by the earth's unrest changed the color of the sky and would for more than a week, the sun did shine. Shakily, like all the other animals who had been so close to the epicenter, Ndovu walked on. He didn't know what had happened, he didn't know what it meant. He knew only to walk on, and he and his few companions came to the river. It had ceased the sloshing back and forth between its banks, and Ndovu drank. All around, birds and mammals were looking for their young, and the scavengers feasted.

At dusk of that terrible day Ndovu, No Tusks and Trekker, and the other pitiful remnants of the small herd were about ten miles away from the place where they had been when the earthquake struck. Detours were now required where none existed before. Some involved many miles, for the elephants were unwilling to cross places where the footing was uncertain. For days they would continue to encounter effects of the disaster. But for now Ndovu looked back, briefly, and then moved on. All that really mattered now lay ahead.

15

THE INEVITABLE

Ndovu and No Tusks remained with Trekker and her small group for a little over a month. Along the way they encountered other elephants displaced by the earthquake, and absorbed three cows—one with a calf, and two more  immature bulls. They also met a large num- ber of elephants to whom they could not of- fer any solace. These elephants had suffered bro- ken limbs and so could not keep up with a traveling herd. In agony in many cases, they stayed where they were and fed. Many would survive until the next drought, and then they would die. The earthquake, active only for seconds, would continue to kill for months ahead.

There were hundreds of thousands of displaced animals of all kinds wandering in the valley in search of desperately needed support from their own kind. It was a good time for predators, for where there should have been herds with hundreds or thousands of eyes and ears alert to check their movements, there were now often only two of each, a situation clearly to the hunters' advantage. Many adult giraffes with their enormously long legs had fared badly in the terrible sidewise slap and jolt of the earthquake, and the young who had survived the quake but lost their parental protection were easily taken. Even a young giraffe is a mountainous feast.

Gangs of poachers moved in shortly after the quake, guessing correctly that there would be dead elephants with tusks for the taking. For several weeks they worked over the area like the other scavengers.

But soon enough they ran out of dead elephants and started killing live ones again. They stalked single elephants and small herds and killed when any ivory was visible. They hacked out the tusks and took them to burial sites for safety while they hunted for more. Ironically, the largest collection site in over two thousand square miles, with over seven tons of ivory waiting to be trucked out to the world market, had had an entire hill fold down over it during the earthquake as neatly as a blanket, and would never be seen again.

The poachers found their targets in several ways. Sometimes they spotted them from high vantage points. At other times they set ambushes near water that they knew elephants would attempt to use. And in yet other times they found tracks and followed new droppings, footprints, and freshly mutilated vegetation. When they had the animals in an upwind position, they moved in for the kill. A successful stalk could take days to accomplish.

Within a week after Ndovu and No Tusks had parted

from Trekker and her growing herd, poachers picked up their trail and began following them. There had been no particular reason for the two bulls to split off on their own, but since none of Trekker's group was in season, it was natural for them to do so. Now they were without a herd and only their own senses stood between them and the guns of their hunters. As keen as the senses of an individual elephant are, they are greatly enhanced by the herd, made surer by duplication a dozen times over.

Ndovu and No Tusks were alert, for there was the smell of man in the land. Occasionally the two wanderers would cross a trail where the smell of man still lived on the wind or lay on the ground. They would hurry on and for hours be more alert than ever.

But now four poachers, part of a group of twelve that had split up, were locked onto Ndovu and No Tusks. They had learned to read and recognize their quarry's tracks and began learning their habits. In a few days, they calculated, they would know their prey so well that they could circle, jockey for advantage or sit it out, wait upon the wind, and kill with relative ease.

Almost as soon as the men knew they were on the trail of two interestingly large bulls, Ndovu knew that they were there. Suddenly it seemed as if he were tired of being hunted. In a matter of hours it was as if this peaceful giant had turned an important corner. He became one of the most dangerous animals on earth. He became what people who don't understand the nature of elephants call a rogue. Ndovu was thoroughly provoked, and he began stalking his stalkers.

Half a day passed before the poachers realized that

they were hunting elephants who were, in turn, hunting them. No Tusks did whatever Ndovu did, so it was the two of them against the four men with automatic weapons. Advantages could shift in this dangerous game, but it would never be a draw.

Three of the men would have preferred to drop this particular chase and look for more benign beasts. They knew that it was now a contest. For the leader of the team, however, it was like adding chili peppers to *ugali*, the finely ground white corn on which his tribe subsisted. He had slaughtered hundreds of elephants, and it was very simple. Only the walking and the carrying were hard, and spending time away from his women. Now, for the first time in his life the killing might be an interesting challenge. He had never seen Ndovu, he did not know that his companion was tuskless, but for the first time he wanted to kill these two bulls for more than money. The other men, terrified of their bloodstained, scar-faced leader, stayed on as he commanded. They knew he had killed more than elephants. His reputation was commonly known. He was also a killer of men.

Instinctively Ndovu knew that cover was to his advantage. In the open, on broad savannah flats, the men could easily see his enormous bulk for miles, while his own eyesight was all but useless. Experienced hunters make very little noise. In places where the wind was not favorable to him, none of his senses could help Ndovu.

In cover, though, among trees and in places where the ground was broken, Ndovu and No Tusks, despite their great size, could move with no more noise than the very much smaller men would make. In cover the elephants could hide as easily as the men. People who

176

have tried to follow elephants in wooded areas have often been amazed by how extraordinarily little vegetation it takes to absorb an elephant and make it invisible. And among trees and bushes, in places where the land and its plants rise up from the level and create contours and visual diversions, an elephant's senses can come into play. No matter how quiet men may be in such places, elephants can hear them. The difference is that if man and elephant make the same amount of sound, the elephant will hear the man long before the man can hear the elephant, if indeed the man will hear the animal at all.

And as for scent, the favor is entirely on the side of the elephant. Small winds, wisps of air, or almost undetectable shifting currents can carry the man-smell around the trunks of trees and through the leaves, and an elephant on full alert can pick up signals no man could ever know were there.

As for tenacity and patience, those qualities in elephants, at the very least, match their counterparts in man. Another factor is that men tire, while elephants never seem to flag or falter. At no time do elephants have to sit or lie down.

And pity, that hoped-for last minute source of reprieve and salvation, the elephant does not feel at all. An elephant determined to kill a man is as set on its course as a man determined to kill an elephant. Neither, apparently, feels much in the way of pity.

The men knew all of this, and for the leader it was an irresistible attraction. He did not plan to die, and he wanted his companions to survive the hunt as well, for there would be ivory to carry and he dreamed of it being heavy. After that he might decide to kill one or more of the men and take that much more profit for himself. He had done that before. It was all the same to him. As a young man of twenty he had killed his own brother in a knife fight over a woman.

The first night of the double stalk was especially black, little helped by the moon sliver in the sky. There were deceptive, tricky winds, for a storm was building somewhere off to the west, and the men couldn't judge with any certainty the directions, duration, or intensity of the moving air. On the floor of the forest they were quite possibly in harm's way, for without their eyesight they were unable to tell when, or if, the elephants approached, and it was possible for the elephants to sense them and hunt them down. It had happened before, although the action is generally after sunrise when men become active. Men do not do well in the dark.

The men knew too that they would have to sleep, which meant lying or at least sitting down. Their only choice was to go high, and they chose a rocky outcropping where no elephant could ever follow or happen upon them by chance. They pulled leaves together and bedded near each other on a stable shelf of rock, and waited for morning. A wind that climbed the far side of the rising landform after gathering force in the open area beyond slipped up and over and carried their scent down with it into the forest below. The poachers were almost asleep when the voice of Ndovu struck them with astounding force. He had encountered the scent, but now instead of running away, he vented his terrible anger. It happened several more times that night. Ndovu shrilled his mountain of anger, and the men did not sleep at all.

At dawn the poaching team could look out across the open land where the night winds had come from, but they couldn't see through the canopy a dozen feet below them nor anything else but the nearest trees. They *could* see that Ndovu and his companion had not given up the game and slipped away in the night. They were not out on the savannah, over which the men could see for miles from their vantage point. That they knew, but they couldn't see where they were below. Once more, though, they heard Ndovu's scream, and exhausted though they were, they slid down off their perch and resumed the hunt.

Ndovu and No Tusks had received enough scent signals during the night and in the early morning hours to know the direction from which the men would come. The poachers knew the wind was still coming over the hill where they had perched the night before and was coming from behind them, but they pressed on looking for signs. They were just about everywhere, but they gave them no new information. What they needed to know most of all was that two bull elephants were following them.

When the men had moved off to relieve themselves the night before, two of them had talked briefly of their plight. One of them was the leader's distant cousin, but he felt no tie to the bullying, thuglike drunk. They were, the two men noted, as well armed as the leader was, identically in fact. They each had an assault rifle from the former Czechoslovakia and a panga from China. If it became necessary, they would both fire at the same time and kill the leader.

The fourth man was older, well into his forties, and somewhat shy. He did what he was told and took his share and never argued. He was a dull companion, but he was fabled as a marksman and considered a good man to have on one's team. When a shot was going to be a difficult one, he was maneuvered into position to make the kill. Now though, he was tired, bone weary from lack of sleep. During the night, waiting between Ndovu's shrill sounds of rage, he had decided that this would be his last hunt. He had had enough. He had seven children and had not been home to celebrate the birth of any of them. He had often been away for seven or eight months at a time. It was not a good life, and he felt nothing for his companions. All of this bore down on him as he followed the leader deeper into the woods.

The leader took the point, and the other three, the marksman and the two younger men, followed in a single file. The leader tried to peer ahead, to see through the trees and brush, but he knew he had little chance in such thick growth. If an encounter did occur, it would be quick and soon over. It would be noisy certainly, and one way or another it would be deadly.

The leader moved ahead making downward motions with his left hand, signaling the other men to be quiet and alert. He was certain that there was water up ahead and he hoped to spot the elephants there, for the banks of a stream or pond were bound to be more open than the area through which they were then passing. If he could just see the elephants, his quarry—for he knew beyond doubt that the elephants could both smell and hear him—he would have the advantage again. He pressed on, peering, stopping to listen, then moving again. He was tired and wanted beer. Now, though, most of all he wanted to kill two elephants.

Ndovu and No Tusks also moved in single file, Ndovu in the lead, on almost the exact same track the men were using. It was an established game trail, which was one reason the leader was certain that it must lead to water. The bulls were about three hundred feet behind the men, and although the wind was not in their favor, for it was behind them too, Ndovu was able to follow the scent trail the men left behind. The men had not bathed in weeks and their odor was very strong. Ndovu could also detect very clearly the unmistakable odor of gun oil. He was able to stay directly behind the men without any difficulty at all.

One sound for which there is no counterpart in nature is that of metal against metal. The leader, the marksman, and the two younger men had the metal they carried isolated, wrapped in rags, fixed so that there could be no sharp clanging at all. Still, Ndovu could hear the men ahead. The heaviest of them, the leader, weighed one hundred sixty pounds but made more noise with his feet than No Tusks, who weighed almost five tons, made walking just behind him. The men were barefoot, but still, they were noisier, and there were four of them to listen to.

The leader didn't suspect the elephants were behind them, so sure was he that water and thus the elephants were just ahead. The trees seemed to be thinning somewhat. At one point he thought he saw movement, and in fact, he did—a solitary, woodland antelope, a bongo, was moving out of his way. He went down on one knee and signaled the men behind him to do the same. His orders were followed, but at that moment Ndovu burst through the bushes and bellowed. The leader turned in time to see the marksman start to sprint past him instead of turning to fire. Furious, he swung his Kalashnikov gun in an arc, released a burst directly into the marksman's chest, and then spun to fire directly into Ndovu's forehead as the massive animal bore down on him. His shots into the marksman were the last he would ever fire. Ndovu impaled the leader on his left tusk, pulled free of him by stepping on him, and then knelt, pressing his enormous forehead down on the man, crushing him into the ground. Then Ndovu stood, stepped on the man, and turned away, rumbling his rage at the proximity of man-smell and the awful gun oil scent.

No Tusks was dead. Both young men had been in a direct line to open on him first. He had been raked fore and aft, and several rounds had reached his massive heart up behind his left shoulder. The fifty pound muscle quavered and then fluttered to a stop inside of its lubricated sac as blood gushed through newly rent holes. No Tusks stumbled and bled to death internally as he fell.

It wasn't until after he had killed the leader that Ndovu felt the crushing pain in his left rear quarter. Six bullets from the same burst of gunfire that had killed No Tusks had slammed into him, tearing muscle, chipping bone, and cutting enough small vessels to cause considerable bleeding, although none of the wounds was fatal. The two younger men had vanished, and the shock of the gunfire that had killed the marksman and No Tusks, and had wounded him so painfully, disoriented Ndovu badly. He turned to worry the body of the leader again, but moved on past it instead. He came upon the body of the marksman and didn't stop, but did step on his head in passing, and then he pushed on through a screen of brush and was gone.

The two younger men had retraced their steps of that morning and scrambled up the rocky hill again and collapsed on the ledge where they had spent the night before. They sat with their backs to each other for several minutes, breathing heavily. Then one stood and announced quietly he was going home to his village. The other grunted assent and they started up over the hill to reach the savannah beyond. It would be a tricky, difficult way to come down off the hill, but they were capable of doing it. They decided to keep their rifles until they were well clear of the area and its crazy man-killing elephant, and then, finally, discard them.

In their description of Ndovu as a man-killer the two poachers never thought of themselves as elephant-killing men. They would never hunt elephants again, and within two years both of them would be members of antipoaching patrols. Men who can think like poachers are among the most valuable antipoachers of all. The two would discover that they could kill men, poachers, some of whom they might even recognize from past affiliations, with no more compunction than they had been able to kill the elephants they now were protecting.

❖ ❖ ❖

Within two days, days when he neither ate nor drank, Ndovu, limping on his left hind leg, and in a great deal of pain, reached a marsh where he had never been before. He eased down the gentle slope into the water and pushed on until it reached his belly. As he moved, he squirted trunkfuls of water into his mouth until he had consumed almost twenty gallons. He came to rest and let his hindquarters sink down below water level as he consumed all of the floating plant-life he could reach with his trunk. When he had swept the area around him clear, he moved over and started on a fresh harvest. The penicillia in the water were already gathering at the gaping gunshot wounds on his rear flank. The bleeding had stopped, but the infections had already begun.

Ndovu remained alone at the marsh for two weeks before other elephants appeared. It was Trekker and her new herd. She and Ndovu made familiar sounds and entwined their trunks in greeting.

In the days immediately ahead Ndovu came to know each of the new herd members, and there was no animal among them to challenge him, sorely injured though he was. Four months later Trekker would come into season, and she and Ndovu would breed. It would be almost a year before Ndovu would find an askari to replace No Tusks, but when he eventually did, his new companion, Runt, a somewhat dwarfed bull nine inches shorter at the shoulders than Ndovu, would remain with him as long as the big bull lived.

Ndovu and Runt would stay with Trekker and her

184

Of all the dangers that elephants in the wild face during their lives, none is more deadly than poachers with guns, who kill the animals for their ivory tusks. ❖

followers for almost six months after they met before going off on their own. One morning they moved along a ridge near a river and turned to cross the water at a familiar ford, while Trekker continued on straight ahead. Ndovu and Trekker would never meet again, but there were other herds, other cows, and there would be other calves, although Ndovu never stayed with a herd long enough to witness the birth of his own offspring. It didn't matter, for all bulls and all cows are parents to all elephant young, and that is one of the critical factors that have allowed elephants to survive in our time.

AFTERWORD

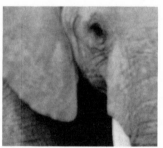

We do not always want to reach the crossroads we encounter in our journey through life, but they are there, and deciding which way to go cannot always be avoided. We have come to one such crossroad now— one that involves the ultimate fate of the African elephant.

A major elemination of the species is the lust for ivory. The world will have to learn to do without it in any form, except perhaps authentically antique ivory from animals long since dead, or the elephant will be doomed. There are an estimated one hundred and fifty thousand skilled ivory carvers in China alone. They must learn to work as well with bone or perhaps wood, or go on to some entirely new profession. The same is true of Japanese carvers and those in other places like Hong Kong and Singapore.

What are we to do with the ivory that is already in the possession of traders and governments, and the ivory that will continually be collected from elephants killed for other reasons? Many elephants are simply found dead near marshes and lakes. In total, even the ivory in our possession now is worth millions of dollars, hundreds of millions it is estimated. The arguments about what should be done with it are many and often furious. I have an opinion: I think it should be destroyed.

Selling so-called "legal" ivory, the short-term gains are not enough to justify keeping the traffic alive. We have to learn to not want ivory and teach this to all other people as well. By feeding "legal" ivory into the marketplace, we do two things: We perpetuate the taste, even the hunger, for ivory, and we invite illegal ivory into the pipeline right behind the legal. Legal ivory creates a market where dirty ivory can be traded—that is, marketed legally.

The poachers' ivory doesn't look any different from ivory presently in the possession of the government of many African states. After all, most of the government's ivory was confiscated from poachers. The whole market must be destroyed utterly, or there will be no end, ever, until the end of the elephant as a species. (The Asian elephant is already in deep trouble and has been for some time.) No ivory trade ever again, anywhere. I strongly believe that this is the only way.

In addition to the hazard of the ivory trade, elephants need a great deal of food and space. They raise havoc with water supplies too. They cannot be confined for long without destroying their habitat. In the end we will have to decide how many elephants we want to make room for.

Many factors are tied up in the decisions that are crucial to elephant survival: How much does a government with elephants on its hands want or need tourism? Tourists need hotels and restaurants and other services that bring money into a country. But they come to see live animals, especially elephants. A country with unchecked population growth soon deprives the animals of any place to live. How far will African tribalism allow human birth control to go? How realistic will the world's religions be about birth control in Africa? How much money can the World Bank and the world's banks make available for conservation education? What is the destiny of a nation with elephants—agriculture or industry? And there are at least a dozen more factors.

Oh yes, zoos. They are already the salvation of a great many species and will become so for a great many more. Elephants will not be one of them. They rarely breed in zoos and maintaining genetically diversified herds would be impossibly expensive. Except in that they provide expertise useful to field biologists, and they are terribly important to conservation education, zoos will play a minor role with this species.

There is no way around it. Ndovu and his kind could be gone in a century or less, perhaps much less. It will be a tragedy if we make the wrong decisions or if it turns out we don't care enough to make any decisions at all. The words "now or never" have never more accurately defined a moment in history. That is exactly where we are with this species as with so many others. It is now or it will be never again.

ABOUT THE AUTHOR

Roger A. Caras, a noted authority on animal behavior, was for many years a reporter on animals and the environment for ABC–TV. The author of more than fifty books, he has made twenty-seven trips to Africa to study elephants and has traveled to many other parts of the world to study animals in their native habitats as well. He was awarded the Joseph Wood Krutch medal by the Humane Society of the United States for "outstanding betterment of our planet," and has been an adjunct professor of animal ecology at the University of Pennsylvania's School of Veterinary Medicine. Mr. Caras is also the president of the ASPCA.